Successful Acquisition of Unquoted Companies

Fourth Edition

To Gavin . . . a natural leader

Successful Acquisition of Unquoted Companies

A Practical Guide

Fourth Edition

Barrie Pearson
of Livingstone Guarantee plc

Gower

First edition published 1983. Second edition 1986. Third edition 1989.

This edition published by
Gower Publishing Limited
Gower House
Croft Road
Aldershot
Hampshire GU11 3HR
England

Gower Publishing Company
Old Post Road
Brookfield
Vermont 05036
USA

Barrie Pearson has asserted his right under the Copyright, Designs and Patents Act 1988 to be identified as the author of this work.

British Library Cataloguing in Publication Data
Pearson, Barrie
    Successful acquisition of unquoted companies. – 4th ed.
    1. Consolidation and merger of corporations
    I. Title
    658.1'6

ISBN 0 566 08099 0

Library of Congress Cataloguing-in-Publication Data
Pearson, Barrie
    Successful acquisition of unquoted companies : a practical guide
    Barrie Pearson. -- 4th ed.
       p.   cm.
    Includes index.
    ISBN 0-566-08099-0 (hdbk.)
    1. Consolidation and merger of corporations.   I. Title.
HD2746.5.P43 1998
    658.1'6--dc21   98-8751
                                            CIP

Edited and typeset by Bill Ireson
Printed and bound in the United Kingdom at the University Press, Cambridge

100195 4768

Contents

Preface

Management research has shown that more than one half of acquisitions are significantly less successful than expected, as judged by the acquirer but with the benefit of hindsight. Mistakes are always expensive, and sometimes disastrous. Unquoted acquisitions can be more complex and hazardous than acquiring much larger quoted companies.

The aim of this book is to provide a structured framework and a practical step-by-step guide to help people complete successfully the acquisition of unquoted companies and subsidiaries of quoted ones. Prospective vendors of private companies and group subsidiaries will find the book equally relevant because the subject is treated throughout from the perspective of the seller as much as that of the acquirer. Furthermore, a new chapter has been included to offer practical guidance to vendors to groom their business, to create competitive bidding and to manage the whole process in order to maximize realizable value.

The whole approach of *Successful Acquisition of Unquoted Companies* is commercial and streetwise. This fourth edition contains much new material and provides important insights into various aspects of the acquisition process. Since the previous edition was written, the climate for acquiring and selling unquoted companies has changed quite markedly. Venture capitalists have emerged as buyers of businesses and they are ready to compete with trade buyers on price, to choose the management team themselves, introduce new people as appropriate, and offer a significantly lower equity stake for management. For smaller deals, however, the traditional management buy-outs and buy-ins continue to be commonplace.

Listed groups increasingly use a controlled public auction to sell subsidiaries, whilst private company sales are usually handled using a covert auction process. Earn-out deals continue to be a common feature in the sale of private companies, and an actual example has been added to give further insight into structuring a suitable earn-out formula. So prospective acquirers and vendors must both be aware of how to deal with the issues these deals raise. Due diligence prior to legal completion is becoming more important, as acquirers need increasingly to pay particular attention to both commercial and environmental issues. Consequently, new material has been added on all of these aspects.

The book is directed primarily at anyone involved in buying or selling either a private company or a group subsidiary. It contains the distilled experience of over thirty years spent firstly as a principal buying and managing businesses throughout Europe and the United States for listed groups, and then as a professional adviser working for clients ranging from private companies to household name multinationals. Chief executives, directors, entrepreneurs, business development executives and finance staff will find *Successful Acquisition of Unquoted Companies* provides invaluable guidance to cross the unquoted acquisitions minefield safely.

It covers more than acquisition itself. Indeed, successful acquisition begins with a clearly stated commercial strategy and rationale, rather than simply a determination to acquire. And it does not end with the signing of the contract: successful acquisition involves producing the anticipated results from the acquired company and maintaining a highly motivated management team and staff under new ownership.

Regulations and controls have been excluded from the

book as they tend to change frequently, and out-of-date information is dangerous. Up-to-date professional advice from a solicitor or accountant practising in the country concerned is necessary.

The chapter on management buy-outs and buy-ins has been updated, because these are an established method for disposing of companies. Equally importantly, however, they provide opportunities for the executive team to have management control of the company and to obtain a valuable equity stake, in return for a modest personal investment.

There is no magic formula to guarantee the acquisition of a company at a realistic price, let alone to ensure success afterwards. The book is simply intended measurably to enhance the chances of success.

Particular thanks are due to Ann Wilson, my outstanding personal assistant at Livingstone Guarantee Plc, for turning my handwritten notes into the finished manuscript for this fourth edition. Similarly, the guidance and enthusiasm of Julia Scott, my publisher at Gower, was much appreciated.

Livingstone Guarantee Plc   Barrie Pearson
11-15 William Road
London NW1 3ER

1

Background

Takeover bids of large public companies make front page headlines in the financial press, and sometimes in the popular daily newspapers. The vast majority of acquisitions, however, are of unquoted companies and divisions or subsidiaries of quoted ones. The publicity received may be only a paragraph in an inside page of a financial newspaper, but does not reduce the corporate significance. It is a fact, not always appreciated, that there are several thousand private companies in the United Kingdom with a turnover exceeding £10 million.

The strategic significance of the acquisition of an unquoted company by a large quoted group may be quite disproportionate to the size of the deal. For example, the acquisition may provide a speedy and significant entry, perhaps belatedly, into an attractive and rapidly growing market segment.

In recent years the acquisition of 'people' and 'knowledge' businesses has grown markedly as the business to business services and facilities management sectors have expanded rapidly.

Inevitably, in these businesses the net tangible asset backing as a proportion of the total purchase price tends to be much lower than in a manufacturing company. So, the element of goodwill is much higher. This compounds the degree of risk for the acquirer, because although the acquired company may employ 100 employees, the future success may depend entirely upon a handful of people.

For example, a software company may depend upon the innovative skills of only three or four software design specialists for new products. If these people are the present shareholders, who will almost certainly wish to leave at the end of any earn-out period in about three years' time, this issue must be central to the decision to acquire or not. The acquirer should assess the potential for development of the supporting software designers and the ease or difficulty of recruiting suitable replacements externally.

Equally importantly, the shareholder directors of the target company may be instrumental in winning virtually every new client. Alternatively, client retention may be dependent upon these same directors' personal involvement in assignments. Such situations tend to be quite common in, for example, financial services, management consultancy and media services businesses. In some of these companies it is not uncommon to find that the largest five or ten clients account for anything from 50 per cent to 90 per cent of total fee income. Furthermore, some of it may be project based and will inevitably come to an end within, say, the next two years.

By now, the key messages should be clear. In any 'people' or 'knowledge' business it is important to assess the importance of the shareholder directors, the scope for developing staff to replace them effectively, and the durability of the client base.

A key to successful acquisitions is timing. The reality is, however, not enough acquirers pay attention to this issue. The ideal time to acquire is arguably when a market sector is in recession. There are fewer prospective purchasers, vendors are happy to give purchasers more time to pursue an acquisition and purchase prices are lower. When the economy is doing well and the market sector is buoyant may well be the wrong time to acquire. Purchase prices tend to peak, because the feeling of optimism generates more prospective purchasers – and deals are completed much quicker.

The key to the success of any acquisition is the <u>ability to accelerate the organic growth achieved under new ownership</u>. Compatibility of the management styles and key people in the two companies is essential. Otherwise some of these key people may leave or switch off, and a 'them' and 'us' conflict may persist for years.

If the people who comprise the management and workforce of the acquired company recognize tangible benefits in prospect, it will provide an excellent starting point to achieve success. For example, a successful company making computerized equipment for the graphic arts industry enjoyed a substantial opportunity as a result of being acquired. Previously, the company's exports had been limited by a lack of finance and people. Suddenly the company had access to worldwide distribution and field service networks as a ready-made base from which to expand. The workforce could see the benefits in terms of job prospects, and the acquisition was off to a flying start.

Potential Buyers

When the first edition of this book was written some fifteen years ago, it was quite commonplace for a prospective purchaser to be the only potential buyer pursuing a particular private company. Group disposals of subsidiaries and divisions were much less frequent events then than they are today.

How things have changed. Today, the overwhelming majority of owners of private companies appoint corporate finance advisers to market their business professionally and to create competitive bidding by a <u>covert auction process</u>. Fifteen years ago, if another buyer was competing it would inevitably be another trade buyer. Today, too, in addition to trade buyers, other bidders are likely to include financial buyers or a management team.

Financial buyers are venture capitalists buying businesses as principals. In order to invest in the most attractive companies, venture capitalists have had to compete on price against trade buyers, even though they do not have the opportunity for unlocking synergy which a trade buyer may well have, by integrating the acquisition with another business. To compete on price, venture capitalists have increasingly found it necessary to negotiate the deal first, then choose a management team and consequently be in position to impose a lower equity stake for management than in a traditional buy-out or buy-in.

A management buy-out or buy-in team raises additional problems for a trade buyer. With good reason, many trade buyers are cautious about competing with a management buy-out team. There is a justifiable concern that if the trade buyer outbids the management team, the result will be that the trade buyer will inherit a demotivated management. Worse still, it is very likely that the key managers will have received a sizeable loyalty bonus for assisting with the sale. If they are still keen to become owner managers, suddenly they have the cash needed to invest in a buy-in of another business.

Experienced acquirers recognize that when they are competing with a management buy-out team it is more difficult to obtain accurate information about the business. For example, a group may prepare a current year profit forecast given to vendors only for it to be subsequently disowned by the management of the subsidiary. Equally, the management team may be holding back good news from the group and prospective purchasers, in order to depress the level of offers made by trade buyers and the price expected by the group.

Controlled auctions are increasingly used by listed groups when selling a subsidiary or division, especially when likely buyers include major competitors. From the time of the public announcement of the sale, prospective purchasers will typically have only five or six weeks to meet the strict dead-line for submitting a written offer. Usually, there is no opportunity to either meet the management team or even to visit the premises. Some acquirers are simply not geared up to make an offer so quickly and on such limited information.

Shortlisted prospective purchasers are invited to meet the management team and have access to a data room for 24 or 48 hours before submitting a final offer. Whilst the data room provides a lot of due diligence type information, there is equally a need to take this opportunity for due diligence because little time may be provided afterwards for thorough due diligence. So the acquirer has to devote considerable resources, perhaps using external due diligence experts and incurring significant expense, without knowing whether or not their final offer will be accepted.

Buying a company being sold using a controlled auction requires considerable previous experience. Consequently, many listed groups who use their own staff to handle acqui-sitions involving a covert auction process, appoint experienced corporate finance advisers to guide them through controlled auctions.

Potential Vendors

Quoted groups of companies actively dispose of subsidiaries and divisions which are no longer regarded as part of their core businesses. An unsolicited approach to purchase a sub-sidiary is likely to be considered dispassionately.

In sharp contrast, some private companies have an unswerving commitment to preserve their independence and emphatically reject any approach whatsoever. Only personal circumstances, such as the death or terminal illness of a key director or substantial shareholder or a major disagreement between the people involved, may prompt a change of atti-tude.

Many companies, however, respond more positively because:

- They are prepared to explore briefly any serious approach.
- If the next generation of the family is not capable of managing the business, or unwilling to do so, then approaching retirement may prompt a sale of the company.
- A common problem of the successful and rapidly growing unquoted company is a shortage of funds. The shareholders are often reluctant or unable to provide more equity capital themselves, and borrowings are probably at a realistic limit already. Selling the company, and retaining the management team, may provide a solution.

  When stock market conditions are favourable, there is an opportunity for shareholders to realize some cash and to raise additional funds for the company without losing control. The creation of the Alternative Investment Market (AIM) in the United Kingdom, the European Association of Securities Dealers Automated Quotations (EASDAQ) in Europe and the National Association of Securities Dealers Automated Quotations (NASDAQ) in the United States has made this possible for many more companies. Nonetheless, some unquoted companies are not equipped to take such a step and a compatible acquirer may provide a more acceptable answer.
- Some shrewd unquoted companies will recognize that performance has peaked – or is about to – and will set out to sell 'at the top'.

Reasons for Buying Unquoted Companies

Some companies reject the prospect of approaching private

companies and group subsidiaries because if the shareholders say 'No' emphatically enough, that is the end of the matter. This is true, at least for the time being. However, many successful unquoted acquisitions have resulted from approaches to private companies which had not considered selling within the foreseeable future. Potential vendors need to be persuaded and cajoled into selling, by being shown the potential benefits for the shareholders, directors and staff.

There are benefits to bidders acquiring unquoted companies, rather than quoted ones, including:

- Unquoted companies are likely to be purchased at a significant discount to comparable quoted ones in the same industry sector.
- It may be possible to avoid a contested bid situation.
- An opportunity to acquire a business with proven, entrepreneurial management.
- The ability to obtain more information about the prospects for an unquoted company, given willing potential vendors.
- Where growth has been constrained, a significant cash injection for expansion may produce handsome returns.
- Questions of monopolies and fair trading may be avoided because of the smaller size of company involved.

Reasons Against Buying Unquoted Companies

Whilst acquiring unquoted companies undoubtedly offers more advantages than disadvantages in general, acquirers need to be mindful of particular circumstances including:

- The danger of over-paying for a business which is performing well because it is near the peak of the economic cycle. Shrewd acquirers look to buy businesses as the sector begins to come out of recession, when profits and purchase prices are likely to be significantly lower.

- The risk of buying a service provider which relies heavily on scarce and highly-skilled people to deliver the service: for example, a specialist maritime loss adjuster, corporate image designers or a bespoke software company. There is the likelihood that competitors will quickly seize the opportunity to headhunt key staff and the possibility that senior managers will leave after obtaining finance to start-up in competition.

- When buying a business which was the subject of a buy-out or buy-in, possibly only two or three years ago, making sure that increased profits have not been achieved by taking overly short-term action at the expense of medium-term future prospects.

- Avoiding businesses which are performing well at present, but face serious problems in the foreseeable future: for example, a business which has failed to recognize that the supermarket chains are rapidly becoming the major distribution channel for their products. Other examples are businesses which are simply not equipped to meet stringent new EU legislation, or a failure to recognize that future success requires investment in information technology to create lasting relationships with key customers. The acquirer must be satisfied that businesses are capable of implementing the required development and that the purchase price reflects the investment required.

The Buying and Selling Process

It is important that a prospective acquirer has a proven framework (see opposite) to adopt for the acquisition

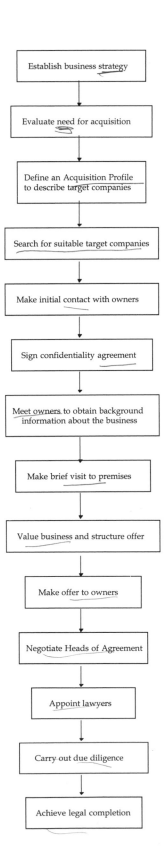

Framework for the buying and selling process

process. Short cuts adopted in the acquisition process may save some time pre-acquisition, but are likely to lead to expensive and time-consuming mistakes later.

The following chapters address the key aspects of the overall acquisition process. The important thing to realize is that to miss out a step is a recipe for making a mistake. Economy of effort and saving time must be restricted to doing less work on some of the stages, and categorically not missing out altogether.

2

Strategic Issues

Before ever contemplating making an acquisition, both public and private companies need to decide their overall strategy and commercial rationale. This demands much more than stating vague aspirations. It requires clear thinking and careful wording. If normal business planning exists in the company or subsidiary, a summary of the plan should be adequate. If not, two sides of paper are all that is needed provided that the analysis and thinking have been sufficiently rigorous. Do not be tempted to short-cut the thinking process, because the consequence could be expensive mistakes later.

The main issues to consider in deciding an effective strategy for developing the business include:

- The direction of the company and key priorities. Both require a clearly articulated vision for future business development.
- The resources available or obtainable and affordable.
- The organizational structure and management style appropriate.

To achieve the necessary detail, a number of specific questions should then be answered rigorously. These questions are as follows:

- Which existing market segments should we concentrate our future effort and investment on? Why? Has the choice been researched adequately?
- Which countries (or regions) should we concentrate on?
- Which market segments and countries/regions do we plan to enter? Have we considered alternatives adequately and rigorously evaluated the new opportunities selected?
- How will our commercial rationale differentiate us from our competitors?
- Which market segments, countries and products should we phase out or withdraw from?
- Which divisions and subsidiaries should we consider selling, or encourage management buy-outs for?
- What finance, people, and expertise can be made available to achieve our goals? Are these adequate? If not, how can the shortfall be overcome at an acceptable cost?
- What threats or opportunities may be posed by changes in technology, social changes, political factors, legislation, competitors, suppliers, economic factors? What contingency plans are needed?
- Are our organizational structure, management development programmes and staff recruitment programmes designed to help achieve our plans? If not, what changes should be made?

The special considerations required for overseas acquisitions are outlined in Chapter 5.

Acquisition Rationale

If the possibility of an acquisition features in the business strategy, then the reasons for acquiring a company should be written down as a discipline. There is always the potential danger that executive ego or personal ambition, coupled with the mistaken belief that bigger is necessarily better will become the motivating force leading to acquisition. Some of the largest multinational companies require their subsidiaries to use external acquisition advisers; and an important benefit is their dispassionate approach, free from internal political bias.

A written statement of the rationale for acquisition helps guard against an emotive approach.

Sound reasons for acquisition include:

- To achieve market leadership or to increase market share in order to become a leading player within the sector in a particular country, and so reduce competition – subject, in various countries, to monopolies, fair trading and anti-trust regulations, etc.

- To broaden the product or service range in existing markets and territories in order to provide a comprehensive 'one-stop' offering to customers and clients.

- To penetrate an additional distribution channel or to acquire access to certain major customers.

- To acquire a leading niche business in an attractive and relevant market segment, where entry by start-up and organic growth would take too long or simply be uneconomic.

- To protect a key source of supply which otherwise may be acquired by a competitor.

- To acquire additional resources, such as a factory or distribution network, more quickly and cost effectively than starting from scratch.

- To enter another region or country, provided that sufficient research and analysis has been done.

- To diversify by acquiring the necessary management, marketing and technical expertise to provide a worthwhile market share quickly.

- To invest surplus funds from existing operations, provided the commercial rationale is sound and relevant opportunities exist.

More generally, an acquisition may be regarded as valid if it is the most attractive way to achieve previously defined commercial goals. An acid test, however, is to outline the specific ways in which the target company would be managed and developed more effectively by the acquirer than the present owners.

Two dubious reasons sometimes given for acquisition are to achieve synergy or to snap up a bargain.

Synergy can be quantified easily with a calculator, but the benefits often prove difficult to achieve. Synergy has been described as a case of $2 + 2 = 5$. For example, integrating and rationalizing the sales forces of two companies following an acquisition. It is easy to overlook the initial expense and delay involved before any savings will result. Additional costs may come initially from redundancy payments, relocation costs, retraining staff and various other items depending upon the circumstances. Also, the subsequent savings may be less than expected because of an unwillingness to change amongst the people involved.

Buying a company at a bargain price may seem attractive. There have been cases where a company has been acquired for £1, together with the liabilities involved. Some of these have proved to be most onerous and expensive acquisitions, and, on occasions, disastrous. Companies available at knock-down prices are likely to need drastic surgery. Success is not achieved by simply eliminating operating losses, which is merely the preliminary step. Success demands that an adequate return on total funds invested is achieved within an acceptable time.

The problems of turning round loss-making companies merit careful consideration. The skills required are very different from those needed to run successful businesses; executives good at one are often unsuited to the other.

So, a key issue is to ensure that a team with proven and relevant track records is available immediately a company requiring a turnaround is acquired. Chapter 11 is devoted to this subject.

A Strategic Approach to Acquisitions

Some companies approach acquisitions as a quick one-off fix, rather like applying rust proofing paint, confidently expecting that one quick coat will give lasting protection for years to come.

In sharp contrast, shrewd acquirers regard acquisitions as a continuous and never-ending process. They watch out for the emergence and progress of newcomers in their sector. Relevant acquisition targets are monitored and a file kept on each one to record financial results and significant events reported in the national and trade press. Key promotions and senior people joining or leaving are noted. A conscious effort is made to meet the chairman or managing director of possible target companies in an unobtrusive way. For example, by making a point of meeting someone 'casually' at a trade association dinner or at a major industry exhibition. All of this requires little time and effort really – and it can reap dividends.

If the owners decide to sell the business by a covert auction, there is a strong likelihood that they will include some companies they know on the shortlist. Otherwise there is a risk that the first knowledge of the sale will be to read in the press that the business has been sold at an attractive price for the buyer. When the owners of a private company are likely to be thinking of early retirement (relatively few wait until the age of 60 before selling their business), an enquiry about the prospects of acquiring the company may be favourably received. Equally, if it is known that the controlling shareholder and driving force behind a business has suffered a lasting illness or a terminal illness has been diagnosed, a sensitive and sympathetic approach may be well received.

Key Point Summary

- Define the future direction of the company in terms of market segments and territories to concentrate on.
- Write down the specific reasons for acquisition before attempting to identify target companies.
- Treat acquisitions as an integral and continuous part of strategic management, and not as a quick fix to address a specific problem.
- Install a full-time chief executive from Day One, preferably with previous turnround experience, when acquiring a loss-making company.

3

Alternatives to Acquisition

An outright acquisition should be the last alternative to be selected. It is tempting to think that an acquisition will automatically provide a neat short-cut way to develop the business. Like exporting, acquisitions involve a lot of hard work without any guarantee of success. The alternatives to be considered first include those discussed under the following headings.

Organic Growth

When a company has the people available to develop and launch new products and services, or can recruit staff, or possibly headhunt the nucleus of a team, the funds required could be much less than those needed for an acquisition.

If the market is developing rapidly, or the company has been slow to enter the market, then organic growth may take too long to achieve an acceptable market share. Organic growth cannot be dismissed, however, as efforts to make acquisitions should be more than matched by work on internal business development projects in the company.

Distribution and Manufacturing Agreements

These types of agreement may provide an opportunity to achieve additional profits and cash flow relatively quickly, for a small initial investment. Alternatively, it may be a deliberate first step towards making an acquisition approach to the company within the medium term, after getting to know it well by doing business together.

In some industry sectors, this kind of arrangement is widespread. For example, branded lagers and soft drinks are produced and bottled under licence in many countries. In high-technology industries, such as electronics, the use of local distributors overseas is widespread in order to provide the maintenance and field service support needed.

There are countless opportunities available, however, in industries where this type of arrangement is at present uncommon. Companies wishing to pursue this kind of opportunity have to take the initiative. In the USA, for example, many small and medium-sized companies have restricted themselves to selling in the home market until now. A British giftware company convinced a US manufacturer that there was a profitable UK market for a patented tableware product. Initially, an exclusive UK distribution agreement was negotiated. This proved successful and today the product is manufactured in the UK by a joint venture company.

Some companies are understandably wary of distributing products to be sold under the manufacturer's brand name. There is always the possibility that the distribution agreement may be terminated when sales have been built up, and before an acceptable return has been achieved, and that the manufacturer will then take over the overseas distribution. Rather than reject an opportunity for this reason, agreements should be negotiated which are equitable to both parties. A key feature should be a reasonable length of agreement, and an adequate period of notice required for termination by either party. This provides both sides with the time required to achieve an acceptable financial return and to make alternative arrangements should the need occur.

Strategic Alliance

In the context of this book, a strategic alliance is simply regarded as an important business development initiative carried out in conjunction with another organization, without involving any investment in or change of equity ownership – at least initially.

For example, two car manufacturers decide to form a strategic alliance to develop a new range of car engines which each manufacturer would use in their own model range. In these circumstances, it is commonplace for investment, management, staff and other resources to be contributed and shared by both companies.

Another form of strategic alliance could be to fund a dedicated research team in a university which is recognized as a centre of excellence within the industry sector, to develop a new process, technology or product. The 'partnership' may include using the developments for academic purposes and publication in due course, provided that the commercial interests of the funding partner are adequately protected.

Equally, outsourcing could be a form of strategic alliance which achieves an important business development goal and avoids the need to invest in equity or to acquire a company. For example, some professional bodies wishing to offer conferences and training courses to their members and non-members have outsourced the operation to a specialist conference and course organization on a joint profit sharing basis.

It is a fact that a number of strategic alliances have developed into one partner taking a minority equity stake in the other (or in some countries a cross share holding has taken place) and eventually to an outright acquisition. This does not in any way negate the benefit of strategic alliances. The outcome has been an acquisition of a business or activity which was already successful with people who are known to be compatible. The risk of failure, therefore, should be greatly reduced.

A Minority Equity Stake

Acquiring a minority equity stake is recommended only in specific circumstances. The danger which must be avoided is being 'locked' into an unlisted company without management control, or even significant influence. In such a case the only available way to realize the investment may be to offer the minority equity stake for purchase by the other shareholders. There can be no guarantee that they will be prepared to buy the equity, and the price offered may be downright unattractive or unacceptable.

A minority stake may be appropriate when purchasing in a country where one has only limited knowledge of the cultural, social and management customs. If a minority stake is acquired the purchase should provide:

- Immediate board representation to enable the purchaser the opportunity to learn more about the country and the business from within, and to influence future development.
- An option to acquire either majority or outright control within a given period and at a prescribed price or valuation formula.

In some countries, legislation demands that foreign companies are restricted to minority equity stakes in certain industries. Provided management control can be achieved, this may be better than rejecting the opportunity altogether. Another key factor in the decision may be the ability or otherwise to repatriate funds.

One reason to acquire and retain only a minority stake may be to secure distribution outlets. For example, in some countries an oil company may acquire a minority equity stake in several commercial oil distributors to ensure distribution outlets for its own products.

Another possible reason for taking a minority stake is to seek some form of preferential treatment from a key supplier. This may be a sound reason, but the trap of investing in a key supplier to avoid the company being wound up could prove to be an expensive way of merely delaying the inevitable loss of a source of supply.

Whenever a minority stake in a supplier is being considered, the commercial rationale should be rigorously examined and alternative sources of supply evaluated before deciding to invest.

A Joint Venture or Consortium

There are numerous cases where the parties involved in a joint venture or consortium have quickly found themselves bickering with each other. Consequently, people are rightly wary of the prospect of a joint venture, let alone the thought of a consortium involving three or more equity partners. In certain situations, however, a joint venture may make sense. For example, where:

- The funds are insufficient to make an acquisition of the appropriate size; or there are no suitable companies to be purchased.

- The degree of risk is too large for the company to undertake alone. Projects of this kind may include oil, gas and mineral exploration.
- An overseas market or project requires a wider range of expertise than the company is able to provide; for example, construction projects requiring specialist underwater work.

If a joint venture or consortium is selected as appropriate for developing the business, then the following will help achieve success:

- Selecting partners with a compatible management style, especially if overseas companies are to participate. If diversification is involved, obtaining complementary skills which will provide the new venture with an adequate breadth of expertise.
- Agreeing at the outset on the management team to run the joint venture. Management accountability could be assigned to one partner or to a team recruited from the companies involved.
- Avoiding undue interference from the partners in the running of the joint venture: this is time wasting, and demoralizing to the management team.

It should be recognized at the outset that the objectives of the partners tend to change within a few years. Eventually, it may be desirable for one company to buy out the others or to sell off or float the business, or even terminate it.

A Majority Stake

When acquiring an interest in companies overseas, there may be benefits in some countries in leaving a minority stake with the vendors or even in inviting a local partner to invest.

The local involvement in the business may be helpful in getting things done more quickly than a foreign company would be able to do alone. Equally, customers may have a definite preference to buy from a company which is perceived to be 'local' to some degree.

When an individual shareholder is to continue as a director of the acquired company and retain a minority equity stake, it is preferable for the purchase contract to provide the option to buy out the remaining shares. Usually, the option would be for a given period and there should be a prescribed formula or mechanism contractually established at the outset for valuation to avoid disagreement later.

Performance-related Purchase

One way to purchase an unquoted company is to buy the entire equity for an agreed sum payable on legal completion. This may involve considerable risk to the buyer and, possibly, some disadvantage to the vendors of a private company where they are continuing to manage the business – it is probably unrealistic to expect the vendors to work flat out for a business they have built up and sold, merely in return for a salary. Other disadvantages are:

- The vendors would normally be expected to sign an employment contract and enter into a 'non-competition' clause. If the vendors have received a large payment for their equity stake, a service contract should not be regarded as a guarantee of their commitment to the continued success of the business.
- If the business to be acquired has really attractive growth prospects within the medium term then the vendors may reasonably expect to share in some of the future success in return for selling the business now and providing continuing management.

One way to overcome the problem is a 'performance-related purchase' – sometimes described as 'earn-out'. This phrase means that the vendors receive an initial sum and additional payment(s) dependent usually on pre-tax profit performance. Further payments are calculated according to a defined formula, normally over a period of one to three years, and very occasionally up to five years.

Performance-related purchases are particularly relevant for the acquisition of service companies. In many cases, the assets to be acquired are only worth a small proportion of the purchase consideration. The real assets of the business are key fee or revenue earners who may leave, with the consequent loss of valuable clients and a substantial reduction in profits. In the circumstances, it is entirely reasonable that a significant part of the purchase consideration should be deferred, and the amount payable be dependent on future results.

Acquirers must recognize, however, that a performance-related purchase assumes that the business will be retained as a separate entity throughout the period of the agreement. If at some later stage during the agreement the acquirer wishes to merge the business with other activities, then this will require negotiation to terminate the performance-related deal prematurely, which may prove difficult and require an expensive settlement.

Performance-related purchases offer infinite scope to devise and negotiate a deal. Experienced professional advice is necessary to avoid the pitfalls which may result. The simplest type of deal could be where the purchase price is dependent upon a given pre-tax profit being achieved for the current financial year. The vendors may be required to agree to a sizeable sum being retained until the audited results are available. In the event that the required pre-tax profit is not achieved then the agreed deduction from the purchase price may be either a sum equal to the profit shortfall or based on a multiple. In practice, performance-related purchases may be much more complex. Careful design is essential to avoid undue incentive to increase profits by deferring necessary expenditure or by seeking undesirable marginal business.

Vendors should only be expected to agree to a performance-related purchase price if one of them has a service contract to continue as managing director of the company throughout the period in which payments are to be calculated. Otherwise the vendors are likely to regard the performance-related payments as outside of their control.

Many vendors are understandably reluctant to agree to a performance-related deal. Sometimes, however, a performance-related deal may be the only way in which the vendors are able to obtain what they feel the business is worth. For example, a company formed in recent years may have penetrated an attractive market segment but only with the help of disproportionately high research and development or marketing costs. Profits may be small, or possibly losses may still exist, and the company may have to be sold because of the problems of obtaining additional finance.

Whenever a performance-related purchase is involved, the contract document inevitably becomes significantly longer to protect both parties. For example, the vendors will wish to ensure that profits are not depressed by excessive management charges or unacceptable transfer prices when trading with other companies in the group. Conversely, the acquirers need to ensure that management services provided to the company are charged for at an acceptable rate. Additionally, to minimize the risk of misunderstanding later, it may be useful to discuss future operating methods with the vendors in some detail and to write a letter setting out any significant points which are not appropriate for inclusion in the purchase contract. An example could be a commitment to open a US sales office next year, and for which adjustments have been incorporated into the profit thresholds for calculating the deferred consideration.

Specialist tax advice should be taken to ensure that no unexpected taxation liability will arise from the performance-related deal being proposed, and that legitimate opportunities have been taken to minimize the tax burden on the vendors.

These are the options which should be examined before deciding on acquisition as the appropriate course of action.

The following chapters deal with acquisition, either with or without a performance-related deal.

Key Point Summary

- Think hard before making a minority equity investment in an unquoted company. Negotiate an option to acquire majority or outright control at the outset, wherever appropriate.
- Evaluate distribution and manufacturing agreements or strategic alliances as a means of business development without the need for equity investment, and offering the possibility of making an informed acquisition in due course.
- Recognize that strategic alliances are a valuable means of business development for many companies, so seek and evaluate prospective partners as a means of pursuing strategic goals.
- Consider and evaluate a joint venture or consortium opportunity rather than rejecting it out of hand.
- Explore a performance-related purchase to reduce the risk of paying excessively for an acquisition at the outset.

4

Defining an Acquisition Profile

Research has revealed that an average of one person's entire year of work is spent for each completed acquisition, taking into account only the time involved up to legal completion and ignoring post-acquisition management. At first sight this may seem a surprising figure, but many large companies have found it to be accurate.

Some prospective acquisitions will be aborted after considerable effort, and occasionally not until the final negotiation stage or even as a result of unacceptable due diligence findings. Also, completing an acquisition usually involves several people from the acquiring company, and there is too the expense of using outside advisers.

The aim must be to minimize abortive effort from the outset. It is essential that subsidiary company and divisional management are not allowed to pursue a specific acquisition candidate without board approval in principle. An approved Acquisition Profile is a key factor in helping to avoid unnecessary effort.

An Acquisition Profile is simply a written description of the important features required in a company to be acquired. It is a valuable aid to clear thinking, and should be signed by the appropriate director to authorize work to proceed. Two sides of paper are adequate to give a description which will focus the search for suitable companies. This means that companies which clearly fall outside the Acquisition Profile will be rejected with a minimum of time and effort.

The Acquisition Profile should describe both quantitative and qualitative features which are important to the acquiring company, even if some of them are subjective. For example, it may be considered essential for the existing managing director of any business to be acquired to continue running the business following the acquisition.

The content of an Acquisition Profile should include a brief description of the acquisition target in terms of:

- Market segments, products, services
- Commercial rationale
- Maximum cash available for acquisition
- Maximum total purchase consideration
- Minimum size
- Minimum profitability
- Management and management style
- Location
- Key requirements for success
- Financial return to be achieved

Each of these items is described below to provide a basis for writing an Acquisition Profile.

Market Segments, Products and Services

A vague description, such as 'leisure' or 'electronics', is almost certain to result in wasted effort when searching for companies for acquisition. More importantly, a vague description probably reflects a lack of clear thinking within the acquiring company and could well result in acquiring an unsuitable company.

'Leisure' embraces countless possibilities. For example, after much wasted effort and delay, one company was helped to redefine the business description previously expressed simply as 'A customer attraction for short-stay visitors.' The new description was, 'A theme park for day visitors providing active participation and capable of replicating on several sites throughout Europe and beyond.' This was clear-cut and as a result led to a successful acquisition.

Commercial Rationale

Many companies do not define the commercial rationale with sufficient clarity to focus the acquisition search. It is important to describe the commercial rationale of the business clearly, so that suitable acquisition targets are quickly recognizable. Equally, considerable thought should be given to define the way in which the target company is differentiated from other companies in the sector. For example, one overseas group set out to acquire a car park management company which focused on public sector clients and provided them with a profit-sharing agreement by introducing car park charges to individual users under a medium-term contractual agreement.

Maximum Cash Available for Acquisition

This should take into account any cash requirements of the existing business and the likely needs of the acquisition over the next two years, which often tend to be underestimated.

Maximum Total Purchase Consideration

If shares and/or some form of loan stock are to be offered

for part payment of an acquisition, it is important to decide the maximum amount of 'paper' which should be issued.

In a group where financing is usually handled at head office, it is essential that a subsidiary or division should obtain approval of the maximum purchase consideration to be made available at the outset. The amount of funds to be provided to one subsidiary for acquisition is a matter requiring main board approval. The subsidiary cannot assume that the funds it generates will automatically be available for acquisition or that, provided a target rate of return is achievable, then funds will automatically be available.

Minimum Size

Many private companies are overly dependent on one person, or at most two or three key people. This may represent a high degree of vulnerability to the acquirer, at least until experienced management support can be arranged, something which often takes considerable time when diversification is involved. It is preferable that the size of the company is sufficient for there to be some senior and middle managers currently employed in addition to the vendor shareholders.

It is generally preferable to make one sizeable acquisition, rather than two or more smaller ones, in order to achieve a given market share. The time spent in investing and negotiating more than one acquisition is considerably increased. Then there are all the problems involved in integrating and rationalizing two or more companies. Surplus directors and managers have to be removed or accept that they are to report to someone else. Operating procedures are almost certain to be different, and some uniformity of systems is usually necessary. One company supplying the retail trade expected this problem to be easily solved, only to find that to establish a common order-processing system involved a considerable investment of management time and cash.

Minimum Profitability

A loss-making company with a given turnover is usually much cheaper to purchase than a profitable one of similar size. It may be possible to buy a loss-maker at a discount to the book value of net assets, and yet it could prove to be a most expensive purchase.

Loss-making companies and businesses bought from a receiver need the immediate appointment of a full-time chief executive. If such a person is not available, the advice must be not to proceed unless it is essentially still a start-up situation where losses are to be expected at this stage. Equally, it is not enough simply to appoint a chief executive on a part-time basis or to make someone available shortly. The person to be appointed should be involved in the investigation of the business, committed to the recommendation to acquire the company, and able to take up a full-time appointment immediately legal completion takes place.

Ideally, the chief executive will have experience of returning loss-making companies to acceptable levels of profitability. For maximum effectiveness, a suitably experienced full-time financial controller is needed from the outset to support the chief executive.

Otherwise, at least a tolerable level of profitability should already exist in the prospective acquisition; and the acquiring company should have definite ideas of what action is needed to achieve a satisfactory level of performance.

Management and Management Style

Compatibility of management styles is crucial for effective post-acquisition success.

The criterion for deciding which directors and key executives to retain must be their ability to do the job in a way acceptable to the acquiring company. For example, some people manage unquoted companies successfully with a turnover of several million pounds by keeping key figures in their head or at most in a pocket notebook. Budgeting and monthly accounts may be rudimentary. Assuming the acquiring company regards these as essential disciplines, then discussions with the people concerned should take place before any negotiations commence.

Many people managing unquoted companies successfully find it difficult to change their management style and disciplines substantially. The acquiring company should keep change to an essential minimum and recognize that some flexibility can be a valuable aid to successful post-acquisition management.

Location

The location of a potential acquisition needs to be considered from a practical point of view. It is better to think in terms of travelling time rather than distance. A journey time of up to two hours is fairly convenient. It means that people can visit the company and do a full day's work without the cost and disruption of staying away overnight. Once the integration has been completed, however, then the effectiveness of modem communications means that location becomes much less important in terms of day-to-day management control. Location is particularly important during the first six to twelve months post-acquisition if a considerable amount of time will need to be spent on site to achieve the integration or cost rationalization required.

Key Requirements for Success

There is no such thing as a perfect company, and least of all a perfect acquisition candidate. So it is a recipe for failure to seek the perfect acquisition. Two or three key factors should be identified which are considered essential for success. These should be complementary to, rather than similar to, the strengths and weaknesses of the acquiring company.

Whilst the aim should be to find acquisition targets with the key requirements for success already well established, it is possible that no such companies exist or only one or two. This is not sufficient cause to abandon the search. It could well be that there are some attractive acquisition targets lacking some key requirement for success, which the acquirer can put in place.

For example, a retailer with an enviable reputation for in-store merchandising rejected an acquisition candidate primarily because the point-of-sale merchandising was poor. They failed to recognize that whilst merchandising was important to acquisition success, they had the expertise to provide the improvement needed.

In contrast, consider an electronics company wanting to broaden the product range by acquisition. If the research and development skills involved are different from the existing business then a strong development department may well be a key factor for success.

Financial Return to be Achieved

It is desirable to specify the financial return to be achieved. This might be expressed in various ways such as a required discounted cash flow rate of return or a minimum return on capital invested. (The question of valuation is covered in Chapter 8.)

Real Life Example

The Acquisition Profile described below is the actual and current profile of a company seeking UK acquisitions in the construction and related sectors. It contains most of the elements described in this chapter.

Market segments and products

- Products will serve the construction, refurbishment and DIY markets.
- Plastic products should be precision moulded, high added value and serve niche markets. Large volume, low specification and low margin products are unacceptable.
- Specialist engineered products will produce high margins by using technology, specialist know-how or patent protection.
- Manufacturing companies are sought, but a business with a first-class product range and a strong distribution network would not be ruled out.

Commercial rationale

- The first priority is to acquire a stand-alone subsidiary, preferably with an established product brand name.
- Smaller acquisitions are relevant to bolt-on to existing subsidiaries, provided that the products complement and do not duplicate the existing ones.

Maximum cash available and purchase consideration

- Up to £25 million is available to acquire a stand-alone subsidiary.
- Bolt-on acquisitions are likely to have minimum current year turnover of £4 million, and profitability is less important provided there is the opportunity to enhance pre-tax profits of the existing subsidiary by £500,000 or more within two years post-acquisition.

Management and management style

- A stand-alone subsidiary should have a suitable managing director and other directors to manage and develop the business during an earn-out period. The opportunity to place a financial director from elsewhere in the group would be welcome, and may be achieved by transferring the present incumbent. The existing financial planning and control systems should be well established.
- There should be a suitable managing director for a bolt-on acquisition which will retain separate premises. If the business is to be relocated to an existing site, however, the need for continuing management will be evaluated pragmatically.

Location

- The location of a stand-alone subsidiary is secondary.
- Bolt-on acquisitions should be within two hours' travelling time of the subsidiary company's head office, if separate premises are to be retained.

Key requirements for success

- Products should serve niche markets and preferably have achieved market leadership in the UK.
- Products should meet the requirements of the European market, and ideally further afield.
- New product development should be well established.

Financial returns to be achieved

- Organic growth should exceed 10 per cent per annum in sales volume during the foreseeable future.
- The business should be capable of achieving a pre-

interest and tax profit margin of at least 10 per cent within two years.

This actual example of a current Acquisition Profile is not intended to be an ideal model to be followed. It reflects the actual corporate strategy of the group and their commercial approach.

Key Point Summary

- Write an Acquisition Profile and ensure it is properly approved at the outset.
- Define the products and services of the acquisition in some detail.
- Identify the two or three key requirements for success.

5

Overseas Acquisitions

There is much talk these days of global markets and an ever-shrinking world. As generalizations go, both of these propositions are valid. One must not assume, however, cross-border acquisitions have become so commonplace that they no longer bring any more risks than a domestic acquisition.

Acquiring a company overseas needs particularly rigorous thought and analysis at the outset. It could prove to be an expensive ego trip. An overseas acquisition should be demonstrably relevant to defined corporate objectives and strategy.

There are sound strategic reasons, economic and political, for avoiding undue dependence on the economy of one country. Hopefully, a depression in the home market would be partially offset by growth in overseas markets. For a company with a dominant share of the domestic market, overseas growth may provide the only substantial opportunity to develop the business. Politically, a business which is multinational is less vulnerable to threats such as nationalization.

There are serious risks involved as well: customer resistance to overseas-owned companies, language difficulties, cultural differences, and simply ignorance of local regulations can prove hazardous. An important foundation for successful overseas acquisitions is to stick to businesses in which the company has proven experience elsewhere.

It is important that alternatives to acquisition outlined

previously are examined constructively, before the decision is made to pursue an acquisition.

Selecting the Country

Before an Acquisition Profile is written, the country for acquisition must be chosen. This involves much more than market considerations. Some of the key factors are:

- Political stability
- Cultural and social background
- Economic environment
- Legal requirements
- Taxation and repatriation of funds

These key factors are considered individually below.

Political Stability

The importance of political stability depends upon the pay-back period for an overseas investment. If you are simply setting up an assembly facility in rented premises, then the pay-back period may be as little as two years. For an acquisition, the time scale is likely to be much longer.

The likelihood of political instability, civil unrest, national strikes and local wars must be considered. A number of countries will be ruled out on this factor alone.

Cultural and Social Background

It is important that the country accepts overseas ownership of businesses, and the implications of capitalism involved. Evidence of this may be apparent by the extent to which foreign investors are treated differently from local investors. Some countries offer valuable incentives, others visibly discriminate against foreign ownership. Standards of education and labour relations need to be adequate to support the type of business and the management style required.

Infrastructure, communications and services need to be adequate to support the business. Without these, achievement may be seriously hampered.

The safety of expatriate executives and the lifestyle of their families may need careful consideration. In some countries kidnapping is a hazard, and there is an unacceptable threat of violence both on the streets and in the home. Substantial insurance and precautions for personal safety may be essential.

Business practices and ethics vary enormously from one country to another. It may not be possible, for example, to operate effectively without paying bribes, ranging from the petty to the substantial, simply to get things approved or done.

Economic Environment

The ideal country will combine the prospect of attractive growth in the relevant market sectors, acceptable levels of inflation and a relatively stable currency. In some countries the general prospect for economic growth may be poor, while certain other market segments may still offer an attractive investment opportunity.

Legal Requirements

Restrictions on the proportion of equity ownership by foreigners exist in some countries. There are, too, countries where equity control must remain with local shareholders in certain industry sectors. The key issue is management control rather than equity control. It may be possible to have effective management control whilst only having a minority equity stake; such circumstances could still provide an attractive investment opportunity. Effective management control may require the expertise of expatriate executives, and in some countries there is strong pressure to replace them by nationals within the medium term. The feasibility of achieving this needs to be evaluated at the outset.

Official approval by government agencies will be required in most countries to complete an acquisition. Monopoly and anti-trust style legislation may exist. Local advisers are needed to steer a course to meet the legal requirements of the country.

Following acquisition, there will be local regulations to meet and these should be known at the outset. In addition to anti-trust rules, there may be exchange control regulations, employment laws, reporting requirements and such like.

Taxation and Repatriation of Funds

The investment in an overseas acquisition needs to be evaluated net of taxes. Corporate taxation rates and incentives, tariffs, withholding taxes and double taxation agreements must be taken into account.

It is not necessarily enough to achieve an acceptable rate of return on the funds invested, net of taxation. The rules for repatriation of profits and capital should offer adequate scope for the movement of funds.

By considering the above factors, a satisfactory choice of country should be possible. Equally, it is necessary to check that enough suitable potential acquisition companies exist and that purchase price expectations are likely to be acceptable.

Companies for Potential Acquisitions

Since the owner of an unquoted company is able to veto an acquisition approach, it is desirable to start out with a number of possible companies so that there is an acceptable likelihood of completing an acquisition. If the type of company to be acquired is likely to be quoted, then there should be at least two or three prospective candidates. If only one suitable company exists, regardless of whether it is quoted or not, it may be necessary to offer an unacceptably high premium to obtain the support of its board.

Purchase Price Expectations

If sufficient potentially suitable companies exist an early check of purchase price expectations must be made to avoid abortive effort. A comparison of price earnings multiples for the relevant industry sectors in the overseas country and the home stock market will provide a guide. This is appropriate for unquoted companies as well because relevant price earnings multiples tend to set a benchmark. By comparing price earnings multiples and recent completed acquisitions in the same sector, it should be possible to establish whether or not likely purchase prices will provide the bidder with an acceptable return on investment.

Vital Importance of Initial Contact

Except for the United States, it is likely that there will only be a handful of attractive acquisition targets in a particular country. So an effective initial approach to these target companies is vital. A rejection to an approach, simply because it was unacceptably clumsy, must not be allowed to happen.

Some people imagine that it is simply a case of identifying either the principal shareholder or family in a private company or the decision maker in a group who is authorized to decide to sell the target business – and then writing or telephoning to explore the possibility of buying the target business. In some countries, such an approach would be almost guaranteed to prompt a flat rejection.

Instead, approach a corporate finance adviser in your own country with an office or partner firm located in the country chosen for acquisition. Ask them for their advice on what kind of approach is likely to be most acceptable and what should be avoided. It may well be that by far the most effective initial approach will be a telephone call, followed by a meeting to raise the possibility of acquisition in an acceptable way, by a well respected local adviser. Even better, the adviser would have a reputation in the particular market sector as a result of completed deals handled for clients.

Key Point Summary

- Select the country for overseas acquisition first.
- Consider political stability; cultural and social background; the economic prospects; legal requirements; taxation and the repatriation of funds.
- Check that there are sufficient prospective companies to acquire at an early stage.
- Find out the relevant earnings multiples and actual prices paid for acquisitions in the country and the particular market sector of interest.

6

Finding Acquisition Candidates

It cannot be stressed enough that any attempt to make an acquisition involves a substantial amount of time and effort on the part of directors and senior executives. There is a real danger that the existing business will suffer from a lack of attention.

There can be no guarantee that the reward for this effort will be a completed acquisition. Indeed, it would be unrealistic not to expect that some attempted acquisitions will be aborted for good reason when the work has been completed. This applies to the acquisition of both unquoted and public companies.

It must be recognized that some unquoted companies are unequivocally committed to preserving their independence and will reject any bid or merger approach whatsoever. But such a policy can change unexpectedly with, for example, the death of a key director or sizeable shareholder.

The search for potential acquisitions should categorically not be restricted to companies which are known to be available for sale.

Opportunism is essential, but an Acquisition Profile should prevent the purchase of a company simply because it is advertised or offered for sale; or it is thought likely to be receptive to a bid approach; or it seems to be a financial bargain.

The key factor is that the acquisition must be consistent with the corporate goals and direction as defined in the Acquisition Profile which is written before the search for potentially suitable companies begins.

The step from Acquisition Profile to a 'shopping list' of acquisition candidates may be a difficult one. If the acquisition is to be made in an existing market segment and geographic territory it is possible that all of the companies which fit the profile are known to the bidder. However, if a degree of diversification is involved the bidder will almost certainly not be aware of some companies which could be attractive. Some successful unquoted companies deliberately shun publicity in order to avoid being pestered by potential bidders.

A systematic search is recommended to attempt to ensure that every company likely to fit the Acquisition Profile is identified and listed.

Acquisition Search in the UK

The data on unquoted companies is well documented. Important sources of information include:

- *Key British Enterprises* which lists the 50,000 largest companies in the UK, including those privately owned, foreign owned, subsidiaries and listed companies. It has comprehensive cross-references by standard industry classification code and geographical area.
- Financial surveys published on particular business sectors. These are available for most business sectors at a cost of a few hundred pounds and are a labour saving way to identify potentially relevant target companies by a systematic search.

- Regional surveys of unquoted companies.
- Membership lists of the relevant trade associations.

Regularly up-dated CD-Rom and on-line electronic database services are widely available to provide unquoted company information. The search and classification capability of these services provides an effective tool to carry out a systematic search to identify relevant target companies. These techniques are used primarily by corporate finance advisers and particularly by acquisitive groups. The initial cost and learning time to acquire these tools specifically for one acquisition search is not justified. If they are already used elsewhere in the group for different purposes, then it makes sense to use them for acquisition search.

The database may enable a search to be carried out against a combination of criteria such as:

- Standard industrial classification number for a particular business sector.
- Range of turnover.
- Minimum pre-tax profits.
- Minimum shareholders' funds.

One company recently used Yellow Pages with considerable success. It identified small companies in clearly defined geographic areas as part of completing its nationwide acquisition network.

Advertisements featuring new products and editorials about them in the appropriate trade journals will reveal possible candidates. Trade exhibitions and special press supplements may also be a useful source for identifying companies active in the market place.

Some acquisitive companies complement the desk research outlined above with positive action designed to flush out companies considering selling. For example, the chairman's statement in the annual report and accounts may make a brief but quite specific reference outlining acquisition intentions. Alternatively, the press release announcing annual or half-yearly results may refer to acquisition goals, even to the point of highlighting the search in the headline. Much will depend on whether or not the prospective acquirer could be harmed by competitors knowing of their intentions earlier than necessary.

Press advertising to find companies to acquire can be unproductive and should be used selectively. Advertising has produced acquisition opportunities in a fragmented market when trading conditions are quite difficult. On the other hand, advertising in a buoyant sector when only a handful of relevant targets exist may well be a waste of money. People should not be expected to reply to a box number advertisement. It is essential to give the name of company or firm of advisers, a person to contact and to invite telephone replies.

The objective is to identify the possible candidates as exhaustively as possible and not to restrict the search to those thought likely to be available for acquisition. Published financial information may not be available for some of the candidates, such as divisions rather than subsidiaries of groups of companies. Figures for limited liability and public limited companies can be obtained by a search at Companies House, or by using search agents, although it should be recognized that the latest accounts filed may be up to two years old.

Staff such as buyers, senior sales people and technical experts should be briefed to report on any information or speculation which may pinpoint a possible acquisition target.

Once a list of possible companies has emerged, supported by outline information about each of them, further information may be obtained by continuing to watch the relevant trade and local press. Enquiries should be made concerning the products or services supplied.

A check should be made in *Who Owns Whom* to find out if any candidate is a subsidiary of another company. This would not necessarily rule out the target candidate. Groups of companies often approach the sale of a particular subsidiary in an unemotional way, and it could well be that the candidate in question is no longer regarded as part of the core business of its group.

The search must not be regarded merely as an important clerical job; far from it. The process should be conducted by someone with marked commercial perception. The outcome could be to identify a company which does not neatly fit the Acquisition Profile but is even more attractive. If this happens, the Acquisition Profile should be reviewed. Equally, in some market sectors one may find there are simply no candidates which fit the Profile. This suggests that the Profile has been defined too tightly, or that no initial check was made to establish that enough potential candidates exist. The Profile must be reviewed and modified to reflect the actual situation.

The end result of the search is a 'shopping list' of acquisition candidates, perhaps categorized into a preferred short-list and a reserve-list. At this stage, no approach should have been made to any candidates.

Acquisition Search Overseas

In acquiring companies overseas, the approach is similar to that described above, but the problem of distance has to be overcome. If the potential acquirer has an operation or regional office in the country concerned, this provides an effective base from which to mount a search. If not, the problem is to sustain the search process. In a large country such as the United States, there is a case for having an executive working full-time to coordinate the search in order to achieve success in a reasonable period of time.

The first steps in any overseas acquisition search should be to understand the make-up of the sector, the value for money available and regulatory hurdles to be overcome, as:

- In addition to establishing that a sufficient number of relevant target companies exist in the particular market sector and are potentially available to acquire, it is important to know the dominant players. Their market strength might be such that sensibly attractive acquisition opportunities are only likely to be found in particular niche market segments.

- It really is important to analyse the relevant acquisitions which have taken place in the previous one or two years to establish the value for money which may be achievable. A simple comparison of the average price earnings ratios may well be an unreliable guide.

- There may be either government approval required for certain acquisitions in a country or regulatory approval needed on a continuing basis in certain market sectors such as financial services.

Only when this initial evaluation has been completed satisfactorily should a dedicated acquisition search be initiated.

The next decision to be made is whether to appoint outside advisers to carry out the search or to do the work in-house. Either way, it has to be recognized that an effective overseas search for unquoted acquisitions cannot be carried out effectively by remote control. It needs to be carried out by people who live and work in the country.

Before deciding to carry out an in-house search, it is well worthwhile to identify leading acquisition search advisers in the country concerned and to meet three or four of them. They will confirm the most effective techniques for acquisition search in their country, the importance of personal contacts and local knowledge, and the most effective ways to open a dialogue with the owners of a target company. Approaches which work well domestically may be counterproductive in a particular overseas country.

If a decision is made to use outside help, then the following section of this chapter is particularly relevant. One important attribute to seek in advisers carrying out a search in an overseas country is their sector know-how as well as their general experience. As more reliance will have to be placed on their work, because the acquirer is likely to be less well informed about the market place than domestically, sector knowledge will ensure a more focused and productive acquisition search.

Using Outside Help

A systematic search to identify acquisition candidates requires a concentrated effort for a short period of time, usually between about two to four months. Except for the larger and more acquisitive companies, it is probably unrealistic to create an appointment or team for the search task. The problem is to make a suitable person available without regular work suffering.

Outside help and contacts may prove helpful and cost-effective. There are several sources of help, including:

- Merchant and investment banks and stockbrokers
- Independent corporate finance houses
- Business brokers
- Major accounting firms
- Specialist advisers

Merchant Banks, Investment Banks and Stockbrokers

Generally, stockbrokers, merchant banks and investment banks are not prepared to undertake a systematic search for potential acquisitions on behalf of a client. Where a bank has a specialist corporate finance team dedicated to a particular business sector, however, it may be aware of possible acquisition opportunities which are likely to arise in the near future.

Equally, it may be appointed by the vendors to sell a relevant business. In these circumstances, the task is to convince the bank that you should be included in the short-list of chosen prospective purchasers. No finder's fee will be payable as the bank will receive a fee from the vendors.

Independent Corporate Finance Houses

The leading independent corporate finance houses may be a useful source of acquisition opportunities, particularly if they have a specialist corporate finance team dedicated to handling transactions in the sector of particular interest to you. When the finance house advises a vendor on the sale of a business, then no finder's fee whatsoever should be payable by the acquirer. Equally, the finance house may well have a wealth of personal contacts in the sector and know of attractive businesses which are not being actively sold but where the owners would be prepared to consider a serious approach from a suitable purchaser willing to pay an attractive price and able to legally complete a deal quickly.

Business Brokers

Business brokers range in size from established companies to individuals operating from home. Consequently there is a wide range of effectiveness to be found.

The best of the business brokers provide a valuable service, and tend to handle mainly deals valued between £250,000 and £2 million. Some maintain extensive lists of companies that are either for sale or prepared to consider an approach.

One or two brokers are prepared to research a market segment to identify suitable companies and then approach them. Most brokers work on a 'no deal-no fee basis', calculated as a percentage of the value of consideration paid. So this can provide a way to complement in-house efforts to find suitable acquisition candidates when seeking smaller deals. Although every business broker has a standard fee scale, in practice their fees are highly negotiable. A finder's fee of about 1.5 per cent of the total transaction value seems a reasonable reward for the service provided.

Major Accounting Firms

Most of the major firms in the UK are part of a computerized database network designed to match relevant buyers and sellers. Additionally, it could be useful to notify receivership departments of an Acquisition Profile to ensure that as many people as possible know of the acquisitions being sought. Both buyer and seller in a particular transaction may be charged a finder's fee, if each party has entered a fee agreement with a different firm. Once again, scale fees are commonplace, but it should be possible to negotiate a finder's fee of about 1.5 per cent of the total transaction value for a legally completed deal.

Specialist Advisers

Some specialist advisory companies offer advice and temporary executive help. This could include helping the company to define the Acquisition Profile, to research a market segment, to identify acquisition candidates and to approach short-listed candidates on behalf of the client. The work should be undertaken for an agreed fee, and any request for a monthly or quarterly retainer should be firmly rejected. The agreed fee should be negotiated hard and a large part of the reward should be dependent upon a legally completed deal.

One benefit to the client is that day-to-day management of the existing business does not suffer by diverting executive effort into acquisition search. Also, the specialist advisers may have a valuable network of relevant contacts not only within the industry sector but also amongst other professional advisers and financial institutions.

Key Point Summary

- Make a systematic search for target companies when a degree of diversification is involved.
- Use someone with commercial perception to carry out an acquisition search.
- Brief your buyers, senior sales people and technical experts to report back on information which might pinpoint a potential acquisition.
- Notify merchant and investment banks, independent corporate finance houses, stockbrokers, accounting firms and business brokers of the Acquisition Profile as part of the search.

7

Investigating a Potential Acquisition

Some background research should be done on each company on the acquisition 'shopping list', using information already in the public domain. The aim is to list or categorize the companies in order of preference before contacting any of them. Some companies will be eliminated on the basis of the information obtained. It is surprising how much information can be assembled without obviously contacting any of the companies. A little thought will generate several legitimate avenues for collecting background material, and some examples are given below.

In addition to obtaining accounts filed at Companies House in the UK, it is routine to obtain literature describing the products or services supplied.

Depending on the cost involved, samples of products may be purchased. If the products are sold through retailers and wholesalers, it is worthwhile visiting several outlets to see how point-of-sale display, special offers and promotion are handled in-store. Copies of press advertisements should be collected. Trade press magazines may provide useful background information about the companies and their competitors.

Once companies on the shopping list have been placed in

some order of preference, the next step is to start contacting them.

Means of Contact

The initial approach to the company requires careful thought. If the acquisition candidate is in the same market sector, personal contact may already exist between board members from each company. In this case, informal contact may be possible in an atmosphere of mutual respect. Alternatively, a common acquaintance might offer an acceptable means of introduction.

The more difficult situation is when there is no personal contact between two companies, and this is often the case. Possible means of contact are discussed below.

By Telephone

Most potential acquirers would not outline their acquisition intentions during an initial telephone call, because of the risk of prompting a knee-jerk rejection. The purpose of the telephone call should be to achieve an informal meeting, perhaps over lunch. To avoid rejection at the outset, the reasons for meeting should be given in broad terms. For example, it could be described as a chance to discuss potential common interests or a mutual business opportunity.

By Letter

A carefully written and personal letter suggesting an exploratory meeting indicating an interest to acquire is received quite regularly by many companies. Some business brokers relentlessly mailshot prospective vendors to locate companies for sale, and may not necessarily be acting for a particular client but simply drumming up deal opportunities.

The result is that many of these letters are put straight into the wastepaper bin.

If the letter does not receive a reply, a follow-up telephone call is essential. Acquiring companies is a selling job, not a purchasing task, and one cannot afford to have any approach rejected without a determined effort. It has to be said, however, that a telephone call is more likely to produce an initial meeting than a letter.

By Third Party

A third party could be a specialist independent corporate finance house or a merchant bank.

There should be a definite reason for using a third party. If the reason is to conceal the identity of the prospective bidder then it is important that the third party knows why. The potential vendors may have good reasons not to welcome the bidder's approach, and the third party will have to put forward a convincing argument at the initial meeting.

Prospective vendors may have a negative response to an approach by an overseas company, or have the impression that the acquirer will be prepared to pay an extravagant price for the company. A third party can help 'sell' the acquiring company to the vendors, and at the same time underline that any offer will not be unrealistically high.

One reason for using a third party is simply to save executive time. The company may wish the initial approach and an exploratory meeting to be carried out by a third party, so that their executives only become involved when it is established that a company on the shopping list is prepared to consider acquisition.

The chances of achieving an exploratory meeting are usually increased either by naming the client at the outset or by saying that the identity will be revealed immediately at the initial meeting.

For many companies seeking acquisitions, there is a

scarcity of relevant businesses to acquire. So it is essential that a premature rejection by any acquisition target is avoided wherever possible. Some acquirers recognize that certain specialist advisers have developed a particular ability to cajole prospective vendors into agreeing to an exploratory meeting, and use such a third party simply to enhance their chances of success.

When either a listed group or an unquoted company receives an approach, even if totally unexpected, it should be considered seriously and constructively before making any response. There is nothing to be lost by agreeing to an exploratory meeting. In some cases acquisition has been rejected emphatically but some mutual and profitable business opportunity has resulted. Before this meeting, however, the vendors should have collected background information about the potential bidder and may have had a brief discussion with their professional advisers to gain some insight into the reason for and approach to acquisition.

Whom to Contact

When wishing to acquire the subsidiary of a group, it is strongly recommended that the approach is made at group level. If contact is made with the subsidiary initially, it may simply put the idea of a management buy-out into the minds of the executive personnel.

The person to contact in a large group is not necessarily the chief executive. His or her secretary should be able to suggest the individual authorized to make a decision to dispose of the target business.

When approaching an unquoted company, the managing director may be the wrong person to contact. It is essential to contact the controlling or largest shareholder. If there is an institutional shareholder, it may be able to offer advice on whom you should contact within the company.

Exploratory Meetings

Where the exploratory visit is made by a third party, this may provide an opportunity to outline key aspects of what the prospective bidder has in mind. For example, the bidder may regard it as essential that the key directors are happy to continue running the business and to sign service contracts. Alternatively, if the bidder regards a performance-related earn-out deal to be essential then the idea should be introduced to the potential vendors as soon as possible.

The first meeting between the principals is of crucial importance. Unless and until a mutual rapport, trust and respect are beginning to be established, any other progress is largely illusory. There may be an immediate recognition by the prospective vendors of a worthwhile opportunity with tangible benefits for both parties. More likely, however, this stage of coming together will take several weeks or possibly several months. In some cases, a company has literally taken longer than a year, or even years, to systematically cajole the owners of a business of strategic significance to explore the possibility of a sale.

The prospective vendors may state that they are not prepared to consider a sale for, say, another two years so that they are able to realize anticipated success. This could be a suitable occasion to suggest a performance-related purchase as a way to avoid delay by rewarding the vendors for future success. Whatever happens, the essential result of the initial meetings is that both sides should feel happy to resume a dialogue at some time in the future. The vendors may wish to consider other potential bidders, but may not actually say so. If the bidder appears to be too eager then progress is likely to be one step forward and two steps back.

The purpose of the exploratory stage is to agree in principle that both companies wish to pursue the possibility of acquisition seriously. To avoid abortive effort, tentative agreement needs to be reached on several issues.

Broad price expectations need to be compatible, although

it is difficult for the bidder to make a definite offer until an initial investigation of the company has been completed. The type of deal, particularly if it is to be performance related, and the preferred type of purchase consideration need to be discussed. The intentions of key directors with significant share stakes need to be known before service contracts are offered. Any significant changes in management style and control should be explained and discussed.

When this degree of agreement in principle has been reached, the next step is to discuss the extent of information to be exchanged before detailed negotiations commence. The scope and nature of the investigation will need discussion and agreement. Prospective vendors are understandably concerned at the prospect of two or three people spending some time in their premises to obtain confidential information.

The prospective bidder may reasonably ask for an assurance that the vendors will not be involved with other potential purchasers until the detailed negotiations have been concluded. The vendors normally require assurance of confidentiality and may ask the investigating team to pose as customers, auditors, bankers or insurance assessors.

The result of the initial approach may be a firm rejection by the reluctant vendors, or a statement that whenever a sale is to be pursued, corporate finance advisers will be appointed to ensure competing bids are received. In these circumstances, however, it is essential that the prospective acquirer terminates the meeting on a positive and friendly note. It should be agreed that the acquiring company will keep in touch from time to time, as the attitude towards selling the company may change rapidly as a result of, say, serious ill-health or the death of a key director and shareholder. Better still, every effort should be made to find a viable mutual business opportunity or even modest collaboration. At least this should provide a return on the abortive acquisition effort and even pave the way to acquire the company later.

Initial Investigation of the Target

There are two crucial points for the bidder to bear in mind:

- Desk research alone is quite inadequate
- Let the buyer beware

A brief but comprehensive initial investigation is essential before attempting to value the business and to formulate an offer. The purpose and scope of the task must be clearly understood. The objective is not simply to 'audit' or verify past performance, or even the current year to date. The aim must be to assess both the short- and medium-term future prospects as well. The art is that of prospecting for and assessing the quality of the gold ore still in the ground, not just counting gold bars in the vaults.

The essence of a successful initial investigation of an acquisition target is to identify the vital factors for success in the business concerned and to examine these in some depth.

On the negative side, one should be looking out for vulnerable features of the business and assessing whether or not the performance has reached a plateau or is about to decline. On the positive side, equal importance should be given to identifying latent opportunities for profitable development and any undervalued assets. For example, consider a stationery manufacturer selling mainly to individual retailers and wholesalers. There may be scope to appoint national accounts sales people to sell to major chains of supermarkets and speciality shops. In unquoted companies there is a tendency to value stocks conservatively and this may represent a significantly undervalued asset and understated profits in the audited accounts.

Another important factor to assess during the investigation is whether or not the management styles of the companies are compatible. For example, a requirement to operate complex and rigorous financial planning and control procedures may be unrealistic to people used to working in an informal way with only rudimentary budgetary control.

Information obtained should not be restricted to financial data. The scope of the investigation must be wide enough to give an overall picture of the business, covering marketing, sales, research and development, operations, administration, human resources and staff relations.

The investigation should produce information sufficient to enable future profit and cash flow projections to become a basis for deciding the value of the company to the purchaser. Also, an assessment of the present balance sheet worth of the company needs to be made.

The initial investigation should only be regarded as complete when one can comfortably make a firm recommendation either not to proceed further or to value the business and to formulate an offer. In the latter case, it is essential that the recommendation to proceed is supported by a list of key actions essential for the successful post-acquisition management of the company; for example, to appoint a marketing director because there is considerable scope for business development but no one capable of leading and directing what needs to be done.

The Investigating Team

The selection of the initial investigating team is important. Possibilities include:

- Using an in-house team of about three people.
- Using an in-house team complemented by an outside specialist.
- Sub-contracting the investigation completely, perhaps to a specialist team from a firm of auditors or consultants.

There are strong reasons against sub-contracting. The investigation is an invaluable opportunity for the people who will be responsible for managing or integrating the acquisition to gain first-hand knowledge of the business. Also, an outside team may be reluctant to report on uncertain and intangible aspects of the business, although these are often more important than features which can be measured accurately.

An in-house team should reflect a breadth of experience. For example, in a manufacturing business the team could be a marketing/sales person, an accountant and a production/technical person. It is important that the team members have had substantial operating experience at some stage in their careers. One person must be accountable for presenting a written report and a clear-cut recommendation either to proceed or to terminate interest in the target company.

The addition of an outside acquisition specialist to the team merits serious consideration. Such a person is particularly important if the in-house team members have little or no acquisition investigation experience. The outside person can be used to obtain particularly sensitive information, while the team leader maintains a constructive personal relationship with the vendors.

One sensitive area may be the nature and extent of benefits enjoyed by the directors, such as the use of an expensive company-owned boat. The directors involved may object to being questioned on such matters by senior executives from the acquiring company. Another sensitive area may be relationships with trade unions. Persistent questioning, to the point of becoming irritating, may be needed to obtain an adequate picture.

Conducting the Initial Investigation

The investigating team should either prepare or be given a

checklist before commencing work on-site. A basic acquisition investigation checklist is given in the Appendix. To this should be added any key features relevant to the particular business to be investigated: for example, the different official approvals awarded to an electronics company, without which it may be excluded from important defence contracts.

Before the team visit the company, it is important that the chairman or chief executive has convinced the vendors of the importance and the scope of the investigation. The approach should be that the maximum offer can only be made if a comprehensive overview of the business is obtained. The point should be made that it is only human nature to bid conservatively if relevant information is not provided and has to be guessed at. Nonetheless, the vendors are sometimes surprised by the scope and depth of information requested by the team. Quite often they are unable to provide the information and may need time to collate material from the relevant records.

So, it is recommended that the first visit by the investigating team is used to describe the information required in some detail. Undoubtedly some of it will not be readily available and an alternative approach will have to be discussed. The investigating team may offer to collate or analyse information from the prime records of the company if it is judged to be sufficiently important. Some selling, cajoling and negotiating may be needed to obtain agreement to provide sensitive information.

Occasionally the vendors will refuse to provide some essential information outlined during the first visit. If this happens, it may require a further meeting involving the chief executive of the acquiring company to resolve the matter amicably. Until the vendors have agreed to the scope and depth of the investigation required, it could well be premature to commence any detailed investigation work on-site.

The outcome of the first visit by the team should be agreement on the timing and conduct of the investigation visit. During the first visit, it is desirable to ask for copies of documents such as internal management accounts to be studied off-site.

The investigation stage needs sensitive handling. It is easy for the directors to feel that they are being cross-examined and to be embarrassed by not being able to answer some questions. There are times when it is appropriate to back off a particular subject and return to it later.

One should not rely on opinions when the facts are available. Tactfully, but firmly, it is necessary to ask the directors to support their opinions with accurate, up-to-date documents.

Listed below are a few examples of problems which have emerged during on-site investigations:

- An office products distributor – each of the three divisional managers had been given share options which would be worth the equivalent of about five years' salary payable in cash at legal completion. The acquirer was concerned that their continued employment was less certain.

- A sub-contract precision engineering company – the largest customer accounted for about 50 per cent of sales turnover and nearly 70 per cent of gross profit. The company was a major listed company, had been a customer for several years and arguably it would be difficult to find an alternative supplier. Nonetheless, the fact that there was no formal agreement with the customer at all was an understandable cause for concern.

- An engineering product distributor – the group had knowingly built the existing premises on land which had been subject to contamination from the use of the site as a dump for some mildly radioactive waste. The group had taken expert advice and spent a considerable amount of money to ensure adequate protection and safeguards. This caused considerable concern, however, to the venture capitalist funding the management buy-out.

- A precision engineering manufacturer – an Inland Revenue investigation had just commenced which involved not only significant issues concerning benefits in kind, but also certain payments for overseas consultancy work which was being regarded as tax evasion.
- An electronics company – dependent on a licence agreement to use a competitor's patented process for the major product range; and a renewal of the licence needed to be negotiated within eighteen months.
- A trade distributor – without any written agreement with the major supplier to the business covering the exclusive distribution rights for the UK.
- A software company – with nearly 30 managers and sales people, having negotiated an endless variety of individual incentive schemes, mostly without an upper limit.

Clearly, most of the above examples would influence the amount one would be prepared to pay for the business in question, or in some circumstances would rule out the acquisition altogether.

Detailed note-taking by each member is essential. Relying on memory is unacceptable. Gaps in knowledge, inconsistencies in the information provided and requirements for further data must be identified.

Formal profit and cash flow projections for more than the current year are uncommon in private companies. It may be appropriate to ask the directors to construct a profit forecast for the next financial year and to give broad sales projections for the following two or three years. The information and assumptions used as the basis for these forecasts must be known. Then the team should prepare their own profit and cash flow forecasts off-site, reflecting their own assumptions and the impact of any changes to be introduced under new ownership.

The presentation of the report to the directors of the

acquiring company needs thought. One method recommended is to circulate the report and then for the team to give an overhead slide presentation to the board. This should be followed by rigorous questioning of the team by board members.

If the decision is to proceed with negotiations to purchase the business, the next step is to formulate an offer based on a valuation of the business.

When the heads of agreement have been negotiated and signed, due diligence work should commence. This should be completed prior to legal completion of the purchase. If anything seriously amiss is discovered, it is better to renegotiate the terms of the purchase prior to completion or withdraw from the deal rather than to seek recourse afterwards under the indemnities and warranties contained in the contract.

Some companies simply ask a firm of accountants to carry out an investigation. This is unsatisfactory. It is like asking a builder to build an extension to a house without agreeing a specification.

The partner to be in charge of the investigation should be briefed at a meeting, and the terms of reference covering an investigation of the financial and tax affairs of the company confirmed in writing. The aspects to concentrate on should be defined, and also those to be regarded as outside the scope of the investigation. After the investigation report has been received and studied, a debriefing meeting should take place with the partner concerned to clarify any queries and to gain further insight.

Due diligence work must not be restricted to financial and tax matters. Specialist advisers need to be appointed to address other issues. Commercial due diligence is vitally important. It is dangerous to rely on the anecdotal and conversational evidence provided by the vendors about the commercial well-being of the business. Market research techniques need to be adopted to confirm the commercial status of the business.

Environmental due diligence is essential, not an optional

extra purely for the cautious acquirer. At the very least, it is essential to establish that there are no significant environmental risks and that regulatory compliance has been carried out and records established. Even an office building may have an environmental risk attached because, for example, it has been built on reclaimed land which was contaminated. The attitude that it is of no concern to the acquirer is unacceptable, because it may well cause the next prospective purchaser of the site to withdraw from the proposed purchase at some future date.

To sum up, the essence of due diligence is to investigate any material aspect of the business between the signing of the heads of agreement and legal completion, rather than naively relying on obtaining recompense under the warranties and indemnities in the contract after the event.

Key Point Summary

- Carry out background research on target companies before contacting them.
- Plan carefully how to contact each company to avoid a premature rejection of the approach.
- Check broad price expectations are compatible before doing an on-site investigation.
- Include in the investigation team those who will either be managing the acquired company afterwards or supervising the investment.
- Provide the investigation team with a detailed checklist for their work.

8

The Valuation and Offer

It is premature to decide how much the company is worth or what to offer until the question of what to buy has been answered. The following case of a light engineering company illustrates the point.

The company sought help to investigate, evaluate and negotiate the purchase of a loss-making subsidiary of a quoted company. The intention was to purchase the share capital and agreement in principle had been reached with the prospective vendors.

Their corporate finance advisers probed the commercial rationale of the proposed purchase. The subsidiary was made up of three quite separate businesses, although these were not designated as divisions. One business was making a modest profit and was of strategic importance to the client. The second operation was breaking even, and it made more sense for the vendors to keep this as it was a major user of raw material supplied by another subsidiary. The third business was making heavy losses and there appeared little likelihood of breaking even with drastic surgery. Closing down the operation appeared to be appropriate as a reasonable return on investment seemed improbable over the medium term.

The advisers convinced the client that purchasing the whole subsidiary was not appropriate and would be unnecessarily costly and time consuming in post-acquisition management. Several meetings with the vendors took place. Finally the vendors agreed to keep the second business as a user of their own raw material and to close down the loss-making operation. This was in their own interest when it became clear that the client was only prepared to purchase the relevant business and would pay an attractive price.

The outcome was dramatically more acceptable for the acquirer. The plant, stock and trade marks of the relevant business were purchased instead of the equity of the subsidiary company. Only a quarter of the total floorspace was required and a medium-term lease was negotiated. To purchase the freehold land and buildings would have cost several million pounds. The relevant employees were offered jobs and the business is succeeding.

Whilst the vendors had the problems and cost of closure, this eliminated a long-standing situation which would have become worse. When the deal was announced, the reaction of the stock market brought about an improvement in the company's share price. There is no doubt that the purchase of the whole subsidiary could have been negotiated and completed more quickly than the deal which actually took place. But the executive time saved and the return on capital achieved fully justified the delay.

When dealing with a receiver, the question of what to purchase should be considered carefully. Obviously, the receiver would prefer to sell the whole business as a complete package. If there are several businesses making up a group, the receiver may be prepared to sell them separately. It is important to explore this. Even if the company in receivership is one business, there may still be room for manoeuvre. In a recent example, the purchaser persuaded the receiver that one product line was of no interest because the product was almost obsolete. The receiver agreed finally to exclude the equipment and stocks from the purchase of the business and to sell these items separately at whatever price could be obtained.

The aim in any acquisition ought to be to buy the income-generating capacity of the business, with the minimum of unwanted assets or peripheral activities. Often, it will be necessary to buy the whole business, but wherever appropriate the issue of excluding unwanted assets and activities should be explored.

Valuing the Company

The essential point to recognize is that there is no single, correct answer to the question of how much a company is worth. The buyer and seller are initially likely to have significantly different views.

Basis of Valuation

The starting point for a purchaser to calculate the value of a target company should be to:

- Project future profits and cash flows.
- Assess the present balance sheet worth and the realisable value of any surplus assets.

Future projections of profits and cash flows need to be based on rigorous analysis. It is recommended that the most recent audited profit and loss account of the target company is recalculated to reflect:

- The accounting policies of the acquirer – for example, the treatment of items such as depreciation and the valuation of work in progress may be different.
- Different operating standards and cost levels of the acquired company – for example, the needs for greater insurance cover.
- Realistic rewards for the directors – for example, lower salaries to bring them into line with other directors in

group subsidiaries; the savings resulting from the termination of the contracts of those relatives employed in the business and no longer required; eliminating the cost of unnecessary extravagances such as aeroplanes, boats and overseas homes enjoyed by directors.

On this basis, the next step is to make realistic projections of profits and cash flows for the target company in current and future years. The benefits of synergy arising from the acquisition should be calculated and shown separately. Otherwise, there is a risk that these benefits will be included in order to justify too high a valuation.

The aim should be to purchase the target company at a valuation which retains most of the benefits of the synergy to be obtained for the acquirer.

There is a widespread tendency by acquiring companies to exaggerate the amount of synergy to be gained and the speed with which it will occur. Estimates of synergy should only be made after asking:

- What specific action is to be taken?
- Who will do it?
- How quickly will it be done?
- What extra costs of implementation will be involved?
- What tangible financial benefits will result?
- How quickly will these commence?

Criteria for Valuation

The yardsticks most widely used to value an unquoted company include:

- The earnings multiple
- Discounted cash flow analysis
- Return on capital employed
- Impact on earnings per share
- Asset backing

It is recommended that at least two of the above methods are used to arrive at a valuation of the maximum price to be paid for a target company.

Use of Earnings Multiples

The price earnings ratio, or earnings multiple, of a company quoted on the stock exchange is the number of years of profit after tax per share which the current market share price represents. For example, if the share price is 150p and the profit after tax per share last year was 10p, then the earnings multiple or price earnings ratio is 15.0.

If the target company is large enough and has the relevant characteristics to justify entry to the stock market or the Alternative Investment Market (AIM), the price earnings ratio that the shares would command should be assessed by comparison with other quoted companies in the same industry sector. Of course, this assumes that conditions are favourable for flotations of this size at the time.

As there is significant cost required to obtain a stock market or AIM quotation, the likely valuation of the target company should be reduced to reflect the cost of flotation.

If the target company is not large enough to be quoted on a stock market, the likely price earnings ratio should be reduced by between 30 to 40 per cent. The amount of the reduction should reflect the attractiveness of the particular business sector and the scarcity of suitable target companies available to purchase.

Some large quoted companies, experiencing a relatively low price-earnings ratio for their shares, would like to think that they will not need to pay a higher price-earnings ratio valuation to buy a relatively unknown, unquoted company than that of their own shares. This can be quite unrealistic. If the target company is in an attractive business sector into which the acquirer wants to diversify, offers the prospect of rapid profit growth and there is a scarcity of suitable companies to acquire, it is likely to command a higher price-earnings ratio valuation than the quoted bidder.

Price-earnings ratios for stock market companies are shown each day in the leading financial newspapers, calculated on the reported profits after tax for the most recent financial year. Sometimes the advisers to vendors of unquoted companies will seek to apply a price-earnings ratio to a forecast of current year profits in order to justify a higher valuation for their client. Unless the financial year of the target company is virtually over, valuations based on a current year profit forecast should be firmly rejected by acquirers.

It has to be said that although the use of earnings multiples gives a quick indication of valuation, it is not sufficiently forward looking to provide a reliable guide for acquirers.

Discounted Cash Flow Analysis

The majority of listed companies use discounted cash flow (DCF) analysis to ensure that future cash generation is given sufficient emphasis in the valuation. DCF is a relevant technique for acquisition evaluation. The purchase consideration for the acquisition is equivalent to the capital expenditure for a project. The net annual cash flow for each year can be calculated by aggregating the cash from operations with the working capital and capital expenditure requirements.

The residual value of the assets should be taken into account at the end of the period of evaluation, in the same way as when using DCF to evaluate capital expenditure projects within a business.

In this way, the acquisition can be evaluated by calculating the percentage internal rate of return which will be achieved for a given purchase price and comparing this return with the appropriate yardstick required by the company.

Whilst DCF is conceptually attractive and relevant for evaluating a proposed acquisition, the risk of significant error in forecasting cash flows for several years into the future must be recognized. Consequently, it is unwise to rely exclusively on DCF as the basis for acquisition valuation.

One of the important benefits of DCF is, however, the facility to calculate answers to 'What if' questions easily. For example, there may be a risk to an advertising agency that it will lose a client as a result of a conflict of interest arising from the proposed acquisition. The 'What if' facility allows the rate of return to be quickly recalculated on the assumption that the client would be lost.

In some situations, such as acquiring a loss-making company which can be turned around into profit quickly, the calculation of a discounted pay-back period may be appropriate. Expressed simply, this means calculating the number of years required to generate sufficient cash to recover the purchase price, after taking into account the cost of interest on the cash required to finance the acquisition.

Return on Investment

Many large companies use the pre-tax return on capital employed as a key measure of performance for each of their subsidiary companies. So it is not surprising that some chief executives use a similar approach as a short-cut method to assess a prospective acquisition.

The pre-tax profit forecast for the target company in the second financial year following acquisition, as assessed by the acquirer, is divided by the net cash invested during the same year. The net cash invested takes into account the initial purchase consideration, any expected earn-out payments and the cash generated from the business or the amount of cash to be invested to achieve the forecast profit growth. The answer gives a percentage pre-tax return on the proposed purchase price. It must be realized, however, that this simplistic approach does not take into account the financing cost of the purchase consideration to be used to buy the target company.

Hard-headed chief executives are likely to take the view that whilst they acquire companies for long-term strategic relevance, there should be an acceptable return on investment during the second full year following acquisition. They are realistic enough to recognize that in a rapidly changing business environment, there is a strong argument for demanding a satisfactory financial return from the acquisition within the medium term.

Impact on Earnings per Share

The rate of growth in earnings per share year by year is a key determinant of the share price of a quoted company. So, if the acquisition is likely to have a significant impact on earnings per share because . . .

- the target company is sizeable in comparison to the acquiring group;
- the proposed purchase price values the target company at a significantly different earnings multiple than that of the acquirer;
- the cost of overdraft or loan stock interest to finance the purchase will depress net earnings;

. . . then the resultant earnings per share figures should be calculated taking into account the overall impact of the acquisition. This should include the effect of subsequent deferred payments to be made as part of an earn-out deal and the impact of the conversion of any convertible loan stock issued as purchase consideration.

Asset Backing

The asset backing of the target company, taking into account the estimated market values for land and buildings, should be calculated as a percentage of the purchase price. For a service company such as an insurance broker, estate agency, sales promotion consultancy or computer software house, the asset backing as percentage of the purchase price may well be less than 25 per cent.

If the bidder has a strong asset backing and is looking for earnings growth, then an acquisition providing considerably lower asset backing may not be especially important, provided that the overall dilution of asset backing is not excessive. It must be realized, however, that the future success of a service company employing, say, 150 people may be unduly dependent on the continued commitment of a mere handful of the present owner-managers. In these circumstances, performance-related purchase or an earn-out deal offers some protection to the purchaser.

When buying a loss-making company or a business in receivership, the aim should be to acquire it at a discount to the value of net assets to be acquired at the time of purchase. If the business is making losses at the time of negotiation, the further diminution in net asset value by the time of legal completion must be assessed and reflected in the offer. The further discount to be negotiated must adequately reflect the continuing losses which are inevitable after the purchase until the business can be turned around into profit.

Other Valuation Factors

The value of a company to a prospective purchaser should not be reduced simply to the calculation of financial yardsticks. The cash flow and profit projects need to be carried out rigorously, the financial yardsticks calculated, and then judgement must be applied.

It may make sound commercial sense to pay more than financial criteria alone would suggest because of:

- strategic fit,
- rarity value or uniqueness,
- defensive need.

An example of strategic fit would be where a chain of retail outlets was weak in a high-growth region of the country and one particular target company existed which would meet the need. Rarity value, which in the extreme case could amount to uniqueness, could be in an attractive niche market such as the provision of specialist computer training courses where the market leader is an unquoted company.

A defensive need could be where a natural product market leader is faced with the threat of a patented, biotechnologically produced low-cost alternative from an unquoted company. In these circumstances, the purchase price needed to acquire the company should be evaluated in terms of the aggregate impact. This means assessing the purchase price on the basis of the sum of the incremental profits and cash flow which will result if the acquisition is made and the decrease which will occur if the target company remains independent.

Worth to the Vendors

Some vendors argue, understandably, that the worth of their company is simply the highest sum, net of tax, obtainable from any potential bidder. An investigation of 'comparable' acquisitions reported recently in the financial press may provide some ammunition to support a higher valuation for the business.

There is no correct valuation. Negotiating experience, judgement, 'nose' and horse-trading skills all have an important impact on the final outcome. Nonetheless, the vendors should use the valuation techniques described in this chapter to calculate a realistic expectation of the worth of their business. It is important, however, not to indicate an asking price until detailed written offers have been received, otherwise the price indicated will undoubtedly set a ceiling on the offers to be received.

There is no doubt that competitive bidding produces the highest prices. The empirical evidence collected by Livingstone Guarantee over many years is overwhelming that when at least four detailed written offers are received for a business, the highest offer will be at least 50 per cent more than the lowest one. More surprisingly, in a significant number of cases the highest offer will be double or more than the lowest offer.

Formulating the Offer

The amount of the offer should be determined from the valuation calculations. The aim should be to arrive at an opening bid figure and the maximum amount which could be paid. It is vital to fix the upper limit before negotiations commence and the figure should be authorized in writing as a discipline.

If this is not done, too high a price may be paid simply to avoid losing the deal. An actual example illustrates the point. The bidder had improved the opening offer substantially to £5.1 million. The vendors offered to sell at £5.2 million. The bidder was not prepared to lose a deal of this size for £100,000 and accepted. However, if a maximum figure had been set before negotiations began and emotion took over that figure would have been nearer to £4 million.

Key Point Summary

- Negotiate exactly what is to be purchased before attempting to calculate a valuation.
- Assess the balance sheet worth of the target company and forecast future profit and cash flows as the basis for valuation.
- Use a variety of methods to calculate the maximum value of the target company; such as earnings multiples, discounted cash flow analysis, pay-back period, return on investment and asset backing.

9

Negotiating the Purchase

During the exploratory meetings between the vendor and acquiring companies' chief executives, there should have been some discussion of the likely price range and preferred form of payment. This discussion is in order to establish at the outset that it should be possible to reach an agreement in due course. The wishes of the vendors concerning their future role in the business and the requirements of the prospective purchasers also need to be explored at this early stage.

If the purchasers were determined to negotiate an earn-out deal from the outset, this should have been agreed in principle during the exploratory meetings. There are occasions, however, when it is only as a result of doubts and uncertainties arising from the investigation of the target company by the management of the acquirer that the need to pursue an earn-out deal occurs.

Equally, the initial investigation of the target company may cause the tentative, initial valuation to be changed significantly. Other issues which could materialize are the need to terminate some people's employment, the need to close a branch or depot, or the requirement that one of the shareholding directors should cease to work in the business after the acquisition. Following the completion of the initial investigation of the target company, there is a strong case to have a preliminary negotiation meeting to talk about the broad shape of a possible deal in terms of:

- Factors arising from the initial investigation which alter the valuation.
- The revised thinking about likely purchase price, if appropriate.
- The period of any earn-out deal and the proportion of purchase consideration to be paid initially.
- Broad agreement of the form of purchase consideration.
- Continuing directors, those retiring, and any consultancy agreements.
- The need for any redundancies amongst the staff.
- The purchase of any assets by the directors of a private company – for example, boats and second cars.
- Any other issues the vendors wish to raise – for example, delaying legal completion for a month so that it takes place during the next fiscal year and will delay the payment of capital gains tax by a full year.

At the end of this preliminary negotiation meeting, it is important to agree a date and a venue for the final negotiations to take place.

It should be established that, on the agreed date, either detailed heads of agreement will be negotiated and solicitors instructed or the negotiations will be terminated. This means that the vendors should arrive at the final negotiation meeting fully prepared and with their professional advisers present, with the overt agreement to agree a deal on the day or to walk away.

If the vendors' professional advisers are consulted after the final negotiation meeting, which was allowed to take place in their absence, the response is almost certainly that negotiations should be reopened in order to obtain a better deal for the vendors. It is important that this situation must never be allowed to happen.

Handling Covert Auctions

Whenever a corporate finance adviser is acting for the vendors, there is every likelihood that a covert auction process is being used. When this happens the negotiating approach will need to be modified because the advisers are likely to insist on receiving detailed written offers before choosing a preferred purchaser with whom to negotiate heads of agreement.

Whenever corporate finance advisers are acting for the vendors, they should be asked at the outset:

- When they were appointed – slow progress to date may indicate some difficulty in finding buyers.
- The process they have adopted, how they have selected prospective purchasers and how many have been approached.
- The date they expect to receive written offers – because extending this deadline later could be an indication of difficulty in receiving acceptable offers.
- The purchase price they are seeking – even though the more astute corporate finance advisers will not indicate a figure until after written offers have been received.

The fact that a covert auction is taking place is not sufficient reason to make a higher bid for the company. Equally, before submitting a written offer, a preliminary 'negotiation' meeting should take place, with the vendors present, to address thoughts on broad issues such as:

- Overall offer value.
- Attractive forms of purchase consideration for the vendors, particularly to minimize capital gains tax by structuring the deal legitimately.
- The likely proportion of purchase consideration to be the subject of an earn-out.

- The preferred length of earn-out period.
- Any other key concerns the vendors have, such as career prospects for key staff.

By having this meeting, the acquirer will be in a more informed position to frame the offer in the most attractive way and at a suitable level.

The acquirers should spend time at this meeting to put forward reasons why they should be regarded as the preferred purchaser by the vendors because, for example:

- The cash is available to complete the purchase quickly without the need for a vendor placing of shares, a rights issue or a stock exchange circular to be issued.
- The vendors are welcome to talk to the owners of previous businesses the prospective purchasers have acquired to satisfy themselves that the price negotiated was the price paid, and that staff have been well treated post-acquisition.
- The due diligence process will be limited and carried out by the acquirer's own staff as they are very familiar and comfortable with that particular market segment.

In deciding the level at which to pitch the written offer, acquirers should always be aware that the vendors and corporate finance advisers will be seeking to improve upon it. Consequently, whilst avoiding pitching the offer so low that the prospective purchaser is rejected on receipt without further ado, there is a case for leaving modest room for improvement. If this proves to be unnecessary, then the acquirer has succeeded in buying at a lower price.

Handling Controlled Auctions

Controlled auctions are primarily used when:

- A listed group is selling a subsidiary – and prospective purchasers are likely to include some head-on competitors, and probably financial buyers as well.
- A business is being privatized by a government department.

A controlled auction enters the public domain at the outset. In most cases a press release will be issued inviting formal offers, typically within about five or six weeks. Prospective purchasers must assume that this timetable will be strictly adhered to, and therefore be ready to act quickly.

The first step is to obtain a copy of the detailed information memorandum from the vendors or their advisers as appropriate. Typically, no access will be allowed with the subsidiary company management before submitting an offer, because there could be about 25 bidders at this stage.

Following the initial written offers, usually about five prospective purchasers are allowed to spend a day, or at most two days, in a data room to have access to much more detailed and confidential information on which to either confirm their offer, submit an amended offer or withdraw. Consequently, there is an argument for submitting a full offer initially, because there will then be an opportunity to make a revised and better informed offer in the second round. It seems pointless to make a low initial offer, only to be ruled out, and then to find that the eventual acquirer bought the business for less than you would have been prepared to pay.

Preparation for Final Negotiations

The location of the final negotiations is important. Any interruption or distraction, such as an incoming telephone call, should be avoided. It may therefore be preferable to use a nearby hotel or professional advisers' premises rather than the vendors' offices. A separate room is required so that either party can retire from the negotiations for a private discussion.

Final negotiations often take several hours, so an early start should be made to allow a full day for discussion if necessary. A sandwich lunch delivered to the negotiating room is desirable. This avoids losing momentum in the negotiations and saves time.

The acquiring team need to draft an agenda for the final negotiations to cover all of the issues necessary to produce a comprehensive agreement and to agree it with the vendors. They must have the opportunity to add items to the agenda, because it is important they recognize that they simply cannot seek concessions subsequently. It is totally unsatisfactory to simply agree the purchase price and outline of an earn-out deal, only to leave the solicitors to resolve the other items. If this is allowed to happen there is a real risk that the deal will fall apart before legal completion.

A typical agenda for a final negotiation meeting is:

- Update of events since the previous meeting.
- Retirement package for one of the directors.
- Service contracts and any consultancy agreements for continuing directors.
- The basis of an earn-out deal.
- Service contracts to be negotiated with key employees.
- Company assets to be purchased by the shareholders.
- Leases of premises used in the business but owned by the vendors as individuals.
- Visit to a key customer before legal completion.
- Any particular conditions, warranties and indemnities which may be regarded as unusually onerous.

An effective ice-breaker to start the final negotiation meeting is to ask the vendors to give an update of significant events since the previous meeting. Valuable information may be gained as well: for example, confirmation that the results shown by the latest management accounts are as expected, that the level of order intake is being maintained or that a major new customer has been obtained.

When the acquirer requires that a director should leave the business at legal completion, the retirement package needs careful negotiation. It must be established that any compensation for loss of office is a part of the total purchase consideration. It is important that the negotiation of a retirement package is placed early on the agenda so that each of the shareholders agrees a realistic figure knowing that this will directly affect the purchase price.

Every effort should be made to agree salary levels, compatible with group salary policies, for shareholders who are to continue working in the business. If the vendors have previously enjoyed excessively high salaries, which reflected their ownership of the business, then the profit impact of their accepting realistic salaries should be reflected in the valuation of the business.

The length of service contracts needs careful thought. In most circumstances, a one-year service contract, renewable by mutual agreement or terminated by either side at six months' notice, is sufficient. Acquiring companies have made expensive mistakes by giving longer contracts to shareholder directors. Within a year of making the acquisition, they want the vendors to leave and find themselves having to pay off the contractual commitment. When there is an earn-out, however, the vendors should seek a fixed contract for the duration of the earn-out period, plus about four months to allow for the preparation and agreement of the accounts whilst the directors are still employed. Subsequently, the notice period could be as little as three months.

Certain key employees of the company may be poorly paid by job market standards and employed on only one month's notice to terminate their employment. The acquiring company may require that they have the opportunity to negotiate new contracts with them before legal completion of the acquisition.

Company assets to be purchased by the shareholder could

include boats, aeroplanes and motor cars for relatives. If the vendors are to be allowed to purchase these at advantageous prices, then it should be pointed out that this benefit is part of the overall sum to be obtained from the sale of the business.

Sometimes premises used by the company are owned by the vendors as individuals. Quite often in these circumstances there is no formal lease; the terms of one will have to be negotiated or a purchase price agreed, if appropriate.

In some businesses, one customer may represent a significant part of the total turnover. If this is so, it may be necessary to negotiate that the acquiring company will be allowed to meet the customer in the last few days before legal completion.

Any key conditions, warranties and indemnities which could be regarded as unusually onerous should be agreed at the final negotiating meeting, rather than left to the solicitors to agree between themselves. Examples would be the insistence to have a retention of some of the purchase price for a period to reinforce the warranties and indemnities, or that the net assets at completion date will be in excess of a given figure.

It is only at this stage of the negotiation that the purchase price should be discussed and agreed. A maximum figure should be set before the meeting, and, if a deal cannot be done within this limit, then the appropriate action must be to walk away rather than to horse-trade upwards.

When an earn-out deal is involved, the specific details to be agreed include:

- The period of the earn-out deal.
- The accounting policies to be used to calculate profits.
- Management charges to be made by the group.
- Cost of finance provided by the group.
- Cost of using central service departments – for example, group transport.
- Pricing policies for intra-group trading.

- Commercial features which will affect profits and should be reflected in the profit targets for earn-out calculation; for example, the need to appoint a qualified finance director and the commitment to open a US sales office.
- Pre-tax profit targets.
- A formula to calculate the amount of deferred payments.

If a deal has been agreed, then, before the meeting is concluded, a timetable should be set to cover the events leading up to legal completion. The steps involved include:

- Receipt of the draft purchase contract by the vendors and their advisers.
- Commencement of the due diligence investigation.
- Completion of the due diligence investigation work on-site.
- Receipt by the purchaser of all due diligence reports.
- Preliminary meeting between the solicitors to both parties.
- A date reserved for both parties and their solicitors to meet, in order to resolve any outstanding points in the purchase contract.
- Formal approval of the proposed acquisition by the board of the purchaser.
- Receipt of the disclosure statement by the acquiring company.
- Date and venue for legal completion.

Both parties must realize that the signed heads of agreement are subject to contract and usually to satisfactory due diligence as well. There is no place for celebration until legal completion takes place. Only then is it appropriate to drink champagne with the vendors. Heads of agreement are misunderstood by some people, because these are only an agreement to agree and are not legally binding. Nonetheless, psychologically the vendors may feel more committed to complete the deal.

On most occasions, however, a summary of the agreement, written in commercial terms, is a sufficient record of the agreement reached. It is not necessary to have heads of agreement drafted by solicitors, although they should be given the opportunity to confirm that they are sound from a legal standpoint.

Negotiating Skills

Some people are natural negotiators, others either intensely dislike negotiating or are mediocre at it. The negotiating team should be chosen on ability, not seniority within the acquiring company. Most people working for large companies have little opportunity to develop acquisition negotiation skills, whereas a professional adviser may be involved in negotiating deals every week.

Some general points of guidance are given below.

To Vendors

- Obtain expert advice on the most tax-effective form of purchase to suit your own circumstances. Particular attention must be paid to minimizing capital gains tax liabilities for sizeable shareholders.
- Do not be hurried. Take professional advice before negotiations commence, and use a corporate finance adviser to lead the negotiation unless your team have adequate previous experience of acquisition negotiation.
- Recognize the legal complexities involved and ensure that you choose a solicitor experienced in this specialist kind of work.

- Spell out what aspects of the deal are important or desirable to you at the outset.

To Bidders

- Before discussing the features of a deal, spell out the mutual benefits; the proposed method of working together; any different reporting or authorization procedures; and any major changes to be introduced in the foreseeable future.
- Do not make an initial offer which is so low that the vendors are likely to terminate the negotiations prematurely.
- If the future success of the company is susceptible to changes, such as the departure of a key director or a licensing agreement not being renewable, take this into account and seek whatever protection is available.
- Recognize that the success of post-acquisition management is often influenced by the manner and spirit in which negotiations are carried out.
- Before negotiating, decide on the maximum worth of the business to your company, and do not exceed that figure because it is extremely unlikely that the vendors will reveal any additional information at this stage to justify paying more for the business.
- If no agreement is reached, ensure that both sides feel that they would be happy to resume negotiations if circumstances change. Absolutely nothing is gained by an acrimonious failure to agree.

Actual Example of an Earn-out Negotiation

Earn-out deals are never standard in real life. Whilst some acquirers do put forward their own 'standard model', vendors and their advisers invariably seek the opportunity to negotiate changes to suit their own circumstances.

Nonetheless, the following actual earn-out illustrates some key aspects. The company acquired was a specialist printing company. Legal completion took place in October 1997.

The deal was as follows:

- £6.5 million was payable on legal completion – which represented 10.2 times the adjusted and fully taxed profits of the vendor company in the previous year. This was a fair to full price compared with recent deals in the sector.
- The vendors were offered a combination of cash and bank guaranteed loan notes, at their request, to defer some of the capital gains tax liability.
- The earn-out amount was to be calculated on total pre-tax profits achieved from ordinary activities – this prevented the vendors from receiving some earn-out from one good year, despite the other year being disappointing.
- The earn-out formula produced a lump sum of £800,000 for the vendors if they achieved aggregate profit before tax of £2.2 million during the two-year earn-out – this was negotiated by the vendors' advisers and was a major concession because they were confident of achieving this level of profit.
- In addition, 50p would be paid for every £1 of aggregate profit before tax in the two-year period, subject to a maximum total earn-out payment of £1.5 million – in reality the vendors felt this gave them too little incentive to really push profit growth beyond the £2.2 million figure which would deliver a lump sum of £800,000.
- The earn-out is to be paid in bank guaranteed loan notes – to avoid a premature assessment and payment of the capital gains tax liability which may arise.

If aggregate profits of £2.2 million pre-tax are achieved, the total price is likely to be 10.0 times the fully taxed exit year profits, which is a full price.

Whilst the acquirer could argue that the price will be equivalent to only 7.5 times the fully taxed exit year profits, if the maximum earn-out is achieved, this seems unlikely to happen in this particular case.

Acquirers need to be aware of the dangers of convincing themselves that the deal represents an attractive exit price if the maximum earn-out is achieved, unless they really believe this will happen. Otherwise, it makes more sense to evaluate the earn-out negotiated in terms of the likely earn-out which will be achieved.

Key Point Summary

- Agree the broad outline of the deal in a preliminary negotiation meeting and set a date for final negotiations.
- Have a comprehensive agenda to guide the heads of agreement negotiation meeting to a successful outcome.
- Agree the terms of employment for any vendor shareholders continuing to manage the business.
- Negotiate any consultancy contracts, termination payments and purchase of company assets next.
- Agree any terms and conditions which may affect the valuation before negotiating the purchase price.
- Remember that the agreement to purchase usually becomes binding only on legal completion, and have a timetable to complete the due diligence and the legal work as quickly as possible.

10

Post-Acquisition Management

Successful post-acquisition management actually commences with the initial investigation of the target business by the team from the acquiring company long before the purchase contract is signed.

The way in which this investigation is carried out reveals the management approach and competence of the acquiring company, for better or worse. During this stage, effective relationships should be established with key directors of the company to be acquired.

The negotiations are equally important to future relationships. It is important that the negotiations are conducted in an amicable way. There is no place for acrimony or ill feeling. Those directors who are to continue working for the company should feel that an equitable deal has been negotiated.

Announcing the Acquisition

While the due diligence and legal work are being completed prior to signing the purchase contract, there is an opportunity to obtain advice from the vendors on the most effective way to announce the acquisition. If any directors are to remain, they should be actively involved in the announcement and help to reassure people about the change of ownership. It is important that all employees are notified promptly and do not have to find out from either the newspapers or their staff representatives.

The first day under new ownership is unquestionably the most important. Not only should meetings take place with managers, but equal importance must be given to discussion with all staff. If it is feasible, a mass meeting of all employees is an effective method for communication and reassurance, as rumours will abound.

It is unwise to make commitments to employees about future prospects. The new management may well be asked for an assurance that there will be neither redundancy nor relocation within the next twelve months. Such an assurance cannot be given responsibly in most circumstances, even if there is no intention to take this kind of action. The only assurance that can reasonably be given is that if it should become necessary, there will be as much notice as possible and full discussion with the people affected.

There is merit in rehearsing the questions which are likely to be asked and the answers to be given. It would be naive to think that every awkward question will be identified, but this does not detract from the usefulness of the exercise. Where an acquisition involves simultaneous meetings in different locations a preliminary briefing is essential to ensure that a consistent message is put across.

If there is likely to be some adverse staff union reaction towards the acquisition, it may be useful to circulate a note summarizing the key points arising from initial staff meetings to avoid misunderstandings later.

Customers, suppliers and business associates should be notified promptly. Whilst initial notification will probably need to be done by letter, this should be followed up by a personal visit or telephone call to key people. To avoid delay, the preparatory work involved should be carried out between heads of agreement and legal completion.

Managing the Acquisition

Effective communication with the board and senior management of the acquired company is the first step. It is important that they understand the following:

- Any change to the commercial strategy and priorities to be pursued by the company acquired.
- The approach to managing and developing the business.
- Limits of authority and reporting relationships.
- Human resource policies and philosophy.

Effective authorization of expenditure is essential from the outset. Purchasing limits must be set, and approval given before the order is placed. It is too late simply to authorize invoices for payment; the expenditure has already happened. Approval should be required for all recruitment, including the replacement of people leaving, to ensure that maximum use is made of available resources.

Effective control of pricing is equally vital. Any proposed amendments to published price lists, fee rates or discount structures require the appropriate authorization. Similarly, quotations to be made at non-standard margins require prior approval.

A key appointment is the chief financial officer of the acquired company. A competent person is not enough. It is essential that the person acts in the interests of the new owners and does not allow past loyalties to affect his or her judgement. If there is any doubt on this score, then there may be a case for transferring the person to another appointment within the group, regardless of competence. The situation must be dealt with according to need, not sentiment.

Senior management must be given the opportunity to raise and discuss problems which they feel need to be tackled. They should be encouraged to put forward their ideas for developing the business and improving their performance. Good ideas may have been rejected by the previous owners without adequate justification or explanation.

Post-acquisition management requires much more than simply attending meetings. It is important that the acquiring company has a definite plan at the outset, with individual accountability clearly understood. No time should be lost before the key functions of the business are examined by the appropriate managers from the acquiring company. A programme of exchange visits can be used to achieve the understanding required in an acceptable way.

Financial Planning and Control

The finance staff of the acquiring group need to think carefully about their priorities. It is tempting to press for standardized reporting procedures to be adopted quickly. Effective cash management, together with prompt and reliable monthly profit figures, should be the first priority. Then attention should be focused on short-term sales and profit forecasts. Standardized formats for presentation can come later.

Unless financial planning and control are well established, it is more realistic to defer the introduction of new reporting formats until the next financial year commences. The accountants of the acquiring company need to demonstrate their patience and to recognize that an important part of their contribution is likely to be in an educational role.

Key Point Summary

- Involve any continuing directors in the announcement of the acquisition.

- Hold discussion meetings with directors, managers and staff on the first day of ownership.
- Have a definite plan to learn about the business; attending board meetings is not enough.
- Concentrate initially on the essentials of financial control, namely: cash management, monthly reporting and short-term forecasting.

11

How to Turn Round Loss-Making Companies

A successful executive may be appointed at short notice to take charge of a once profitable company which is now operating at a loss. His or her priorities will be to ensure that the business does not run out of cash and to achieve a turnround to profit.

The approach needed to turn a business round is substantially different from managing a profitable company. As speed is essential in any turnround operation, the executive must have a proven framework for tackling the problem. His or her first impression will probably be that everyone appears to be busily occupied. It is unlikely that losses have been caused by lack of effort on the part of either workforce or management. The problem is more likely to be one of directing effort, rather than of increasing it; in other words, ensuring that people throughout the business are geared to achieve results and do not mistake movement for action.

Making an Impact

The first and urgent task is to ensure the company is not trading illegally and that sufficient finance is available in the short term to enable the company to survive. The existing management will probably expect and want immediate action from the new executive. Furthermore, they will expect the action to be tough. The executive will be rightly concerned about his or her ignorance of the company. Radical organizational change or the switching of key personnel, if implemented too quickly, might prove to be inadequate or misguided measures in the months to come. Nonetheless, some impact can be made immediately, as discused below.

Temporary Help

Terminate all temporary help immediately and fill the resulting gaps by redeploying existing permanent staff. If this causes a real problem, someone will scream loud enough. In the end the business is unlikely to suffer.

Indirect Staff

Insist that the recruitment of all indirect personnel (part of the company overhead), including replacement staff, will need chief executive approval before any action is taken. Review all indirect staff recruitment in progress. Stop all hiring except where an exhaustive check of existing staff availability reveals an unquestionable need.

Direct Staff

If there is any likelihood that some redundancies will be necessary in due course amongst staff directly involved in producing and delivering the product or service, then any recruitment should require chief executive approval. This applies particularly in those countries where staff costs should realistically be regarded as fixed in the short term, rather than variable, because of the difficulty and cost of terminating any employee.

Fixed Assets

Insist that all capital expenditure above a given level is approved by the chief executive. Wherever possible, delay non-profit projects such as the replacement of staff dining room equipment, refurbishing car parks, etc. Ask that unused plant and machinery be identified with a view to disposal, and that under-utilized floorspace be identified so that the use of facilities can be rationalized in due course.

Inventory

Ensure that significant purchases against anticipated special orders receive chief executive approval. Material purchases should be allowed to proceed normally when covered by firm orders or when part of a standard product specification. Ask that all redundant stocks be identified and vigorous attempts made to dispose of the surplus at whatever price can be obtained.

Offices and Office Equipment

Cut back sharply on the redecoration of offices and the routine replacement of office equipment. The order of the day should be to make do and mend wherever financially justified.

Personal Cars

Delay, wherever possible, the replacement of cars supplied and maintained by the company, and keep the authorization of additional cars to an absolute minimum.

Foreign Travel

All foreign travel should require chief executive approval. In one actual example, the marketing manager had arranged a three-week visit to Brazil in order to assist the company's local distributor to expand sales. A request for a visit programme listing the companies and executives to be visited quickly established that no such planning had been done. The approval was deferred until such time as the local distributor had arranged an effective itinerary. Six months later the application still had not been re-submitted.

Where significant costs are incurred on travel between various company locations, it may be possible to make savings quickly by using video conferencing techniques.

Entertaining

Check expense claims to ensure that any entertaining of clients is not unnecessarily lavish. There is more at stake here than the cost of the entertaining; in a loss-making company many employees justifiably feel bitter when they hear about expense of this kind.

The impact of a series of immediate actions such as those listed above (not an exhaustive list) really gets the message across that the decks are being cleared for action. The objective is to make the most effective use of the human and material resources already employed in the business. Admittedly, the impact of these actions is likely to be more important in terms of the effect on employee attitudes than on profitability and cash flow; but some tangible improvement will almost certainly result. Clearly, the turnround executive will want to reduce the list of actions requiring personal approval as soon as his or her values and standards are shared by the management team.

The Programme

Now the turnround programme may be started in earnest. The first task is to understand what is happening in the business, before taking precipitate executive action. What is more, the answers necessary for short-term success are likely to be found amongst the middle and senior managers of the company. The key questions to be asked of people by the turnround executive are as follows:

- What key factors are stopping you and the business being more effective and successful?
- What inexpensive and simple action would have a substantial effect on the performance of the company?
- What extra help do you need to do your job more effectively?
- What tasks could be eliminated altogether or made simpler and more effective?
- What is not being done that needs doing urgently?

Managers are often able to highlight a key problem area or opportunity in another department of the company while not being able to see scope for improvement in their own job. The turnround executive needs to be a good listener who neither takes sides nor apportions blame.

Start in the Sales Department

Even in a high-technology company there is the strongest case for trying to understand the fundamental problems facing the business by examining the sales activity first. Almost by definition, a loss-making company cannot claim to be sufficiently market-oriented. Ideally, every sales employee should regard their job as helping to provide outstanding service to present customers and anticipating the future needs of both established and potential customers. In working to achieve this state of affairs, there is no effective substitute for making field visits with sales staff, visiting agents and distributors, calling upon important customers, potential customers and even important established users of competitive products. Board meetings are unlikely to provide an adequate insight into the sales and marketing issues facing the business.

Two weeks spent in the field represent an excellent investment of the turnround executive's time at this stage. In this way, first-hand information can be obtained about the product quality, service and delivery performance. Price competitiveness, the benefits offered by competitive products, the effectiveness of sales and distribution networks will begin to be understood as well.

Attention should next be focused on the sales office and sales support services. The time already spent in the field will prove invaluable in asking the relevant questions about the effectiveness of sales support. A good starting point is to check how effectively action is taken on correspondence and telephone calls from customers. Operating standards are vital. Enquiries and orders should be acknowledged the same day. Complaints and requests for after-sales service require particularly prompt attention. It is essential to notify the customer of the action being taken without delay. General correspondence, too, should be handled promptly. When a telephone query cannot be dealt with on the spot, a promise should be made to call back by a given time, and that promise must be honoured.

Clearly, the effective handling of correspondence and telephone calls is not a panacea for the sales ills confronting a business. The attitude of mind that creates this type of effectiveness, however, is a prerequisite for what needs to be achieved in the coming weeks and months.

The turnround executive will then want to evaluate other important aspects of the sales operation. At this stage, the executive's previous management experience and newly-gained knowledge of the present business will indicate which aspects require attention. Aspects to evaluate may include:

- The existence of adequate targets, incentives, operating standards, training and supervision for the sales force.

- The liaison between the sales and production departments to ensure that the various customer demands and priorities are met in a cost-effective way.
- The finished goods stocking policy used to ensure a balance between meeting customer orders from stock and the attendant cost of holding the inventory to achieve this goal.
- The acceptance of orders for custom-made products as opposed to standard ones, and the basis for assessing the costs involved and the price to be charged.
- The responsibility and basis for offering one-off, cut-price or discount deals to customers or clients.
- The extent to which the sales people participate in helping to collect overdue accounts from customers.
- The need to make the maximum use of information technology to help the sales force improve the service to customers and clients.

This is an intentionally simple approach, based on finding out exactly what happens rather than installing sophisticated management systems and controls.

Successful turnrounds are usually initiated by executive action ensuring that a few simple but important things are done outstandingly well. Installing some basic management controls should wait until this first stage in recovery has been effected.

It may appear somewhat illogical to investigate the sales activity before tackling the broader issues of the market place and marketing; the reason for this is pragmatic. Even a sketchy knowledge of the sales effort, problems and opportunities will lend considerable perspective to one's understanding of the marketing challenge facing the business. Important marketing aspects to be looked at include:

- Any major products or services in the research and development stage for which there should be a clear-cut work programme through to product launch with an attendant expense budget.

- Business development, including efforts to identify and pursue new products, services, territories, market segments and distribution channels.
- The effectiveness of sales promotion, advertising and exhibition expenditure.
- The liaison between marketing and R&D to ensure that research projects are based on a market-oriented assessment of customer needs and provisional product specifications.
- The extent, relevance and value of market research activity and data within the company as a basis for future business development.
- The possible need for reduction in the range of products/models and services offered to the customers to ensure compatibility between market needs and the cost-effective use of production resources.

The Function of Finance

Time is of the essence, and it is therefore highly desirable that the groundwork in financial planning and control should be started at the same time as the turnround executive begins to look at the sales activity. Ideally an experienced financial manager will be assigned to the business full-time for a given period. If this is not possible, then the turnround executive must be able to give instructions to the existing financial director as to precisely what financial information is required.

From the outset, the role of the finance function is to provide other members of the management team with a service which is designed to make a tangible contribution to profitability and cash flow. In a turnround situation the real need is for sufficiently accurate figures produced promptly. Immaculately presented historical figures may be interesting, but represent a luxury at this stage. Forecast figures are invaluable as a basis for executive action.

There must be a dual attack on both profitability and cash management. While a budget may exist for the remainder of the current financial year, the turnround executive will be more interested in a month-by-month updated forecast of the detailed profit and loss account, compared with the original budget for the rest of the year. Ideally, this will be presented to show both the percentage and amount of marginal profit contributed by each major product or service. Similarly, an updated cash flow forecast is needed weekly for the next month at least, then monthly for the remainder of the year.

Forecasts and Objectives

Forecasts must be prepared on the basis of consultation between the line managers and the finance staff. It must be the line managers' own forecast as processed by the finance department, not an accountant's view alone of what the future holds. With the help of this simple financial picture, the turnround executive will be able to highlight the most significant areas of the business to be attacked first, whether these are sales revenue, marginal profit levels, production costs or overhead expenses. Obviously the turnround executive is seriously handicapped until these updated forecasts are available, and the senior finance staff should be expected to work flat out to produce them, with whatever overtime working is necessary.

The financial forecasts, plus consultation with line managers and finance staff, will no doubt show up a need for a series of *ad hoc* financial analysis exercises, to be completed quickly as the basis for short-term management action programmes to improve both profitability and cash management.

Clear-cut deadlines for the completion of this work should be agreed with the finance staff.

By now the turnround executive will have been in charge of the business for 30 days or so and will have been getting to know the management team. They in turn will have seen something of the new executive's management style, values and standards. Now is the time to set about translating the forecast for the remainder of the current year into firm objectives. Each member of the management team should be asked to present their own revised objectives for the rest of the year, translated into financial figures with the help of the finance staff, and backed by a specific management action programme, together with a statement of any key assumptions incorporated.

These statements of revised objectives should be presented to the turnround executive for discussion, review and approval within a further 15 days. This allows another 15 days for revision and compilation of an overall business plan for the remainder of the current year. This means that 60 days after taking up the appointment, the turnround executive and the management team have an operating plan for the remainder of the year, backed by management action programmes and a statement of key assumptions. By this time, too, the management team will realize that an operating plan is a commitment to achieve certain results, subject only to uncontrollable and unforeseeable factors.

A Close Look at Administration

While the management team is preparing its objectives, the turnround executive should spend the second 30 days having a detailed look at the remainder of the business, including administration, production and R&D. Administration takes priority because in a turnround situation it can represent a very real burden. In looking at administration expense, in the broadest sense, the turnround executive should have value analysis concepts very much in mind. He or she will be asking themselves, and others, the reason for each administrative activity, using the type of questions which follow:

- Is the work necessary to meet statutory, legal or fiscal requirements?
- If not, what detriment would there be to the business in either the short- or long-term if the particular task or department was eliminated?
- If the work still appears necessary, who benefits internally, and is the existing service the most cost-effective and relevant approach?
- Are any administrative departments overstaffed or staffed to meet a peak demand?
- Is there any administrative work not being done which would represent both a tangible benefit and a net overall saving to the business?
- Are costs higher than necessary as a result of using expensive contract staff?
- Could any services or departments be outsourced partially or completely, to reduce costs without damaging the business later?
- Is maximum and cost-effective use being made of information technology such as recent developments in data storage and transmission, direct input and e-mail?

At the end of this learning period the turnround executive should have got across the message to the team that empire-building and status symbols are out. The order of the day is to provide a service which represents value for money.

The Production Angle

The turnround executive may never have worked in a production department, but this must not be a deterrent to taking an earnest look at the activity. In the same way that time was spent in the field in order to appreciate quickly the sales and marketing problems, it is necessary to spend time in production departments and warehouses to begin to understand the production challenge facing the business. Good housekeeping is important. It is not just a question of tidiness. If management and workforce alike do not take pride in their surroundings and adopt high standards, they are unlikely to take pride in the quality of the products and services supplied to customers.

On the very first visit to each location the turnround executive should not hesitate to point out any lack of good housekeeping and to expect rapid action to improve the situation. Once again the premise is that major improvement throughout the production process needs a basic change of attitude at the outset. The turnround executive will constantly be asking fundamental questions: Why? How? and What? The specific questions may include:

- What are the major constraints holding back increased output and productivity, quicker and more reliable delivery performance, better product or service quality and reliability, and reduced inventory levels?
- How can we overcome these constraints in the most effective and inexpensive way in the shortest time possible?
- What should be done to improve the working conditions, motivation and morale of the workforce? How much will this cost? What other savings can be achieved to pay for it?

Research and Development

There is a strong temptation for the turnround executive to

avoid getting to grips with the R&D activity because of a lack of technical expertise. The temptation must be resisted at all costs. It is perfectly admissible to admit to ignorance of the technology involved, provided that the executive demonstrates a willingness to appreciate the problems of and to take a lively interest in the work of the department. This approach will almost certainly enhance the respect that hopefully he or she has already earned. Questions to ask in the R&D department may include:

- Who initiated each R&D project currently in progress?
- What budget and programme exists for each project? How does actual performance compare with the original budget and programme?
- What financial return is expected from each project? What market research data is this based on? What product specification and price profile has been agreed with marketing and defined as the objective?
- What existing projects should be examined with a view to termination?
- What new projects should be initiated? For what reason?
- How can information technology be used more widely and effectively to increase the productivity of R&D staff?
- How can the Internet be used as a research tool to spur innovation and to provide a valuable information resource?
- What is the allocation of R&D resources between basic research, new product R&D and the improvement of existing products? Does this allocation meet the future market opportunities and competitive challenges facing the business?
- What is the current level of sales and marginal profit contribution derived from products emanating from in-house R&D?
- What R&D work is outsourced or sub-contracted to

other organizations? Which projects or specific tasks should be outsourced or sub-contracted in future?

The Way Ahead

By now the turnround executive has spent 60 days getting to understand the business and its markets. Short-term action programmes have been initiated, by requiring firm objectives for the rest of the current financial year from management colleagues. Now the executive must start to introduce more fundamental and long-term change. One important action is to review the organization structure and to decide what changes, if any, are needed. At the same time arrangements should be made to either confirm the selection of each member of the management team or to announce alternative plans. The turnround executive will need a simple approach to organization. The aim will be to achieve a compact management team, with clear-cut accountabilities and the most direct lines of communication possible from top management to every member of staff.

Reducing the Workforce

At the same time, policy will have been decided in broad terms regarding the extent of staff reduction needed. The turnround executive will be ready to discuss the policy with the management team. With luck, no dismissals will have been needed during the first 60 days. A piecemeal approach to reducing the workforce has a devastating effect on morale. Nevertheless, if the situation was sufficiently serious to warrant earlier redundancies, then no doubt they would have happened.

Consideration should be given to making use of temporary staff, short fixed-term contracts for staff and outsourcing as part of a review of current staffing levels.

Each member of the management team should be asked to produce a list of people either to be made redundant or transferred internally. The information required in addition to the names of the people affected is their job title, length of service, annual income, notice period and the cost of termination.

This part of handling a turnround situation is undoubtedly the most unpleasant aspect of the job. The executive reluctantly responsible for this task must do the utmost to ensure that people are treated fairly, and as generously and compassionately as possible. Failure to recognize the need for a reduction can only result in putting the jobs of everyone in the business at risk.

One thing the turnround executive must ensure is that the scheme to reduce the number of staff covers the entire business, from workforce through to senior management; otherwise a top-heavy organization may well result. Clearly, however, to meet the future needs of the company some departments will need to suffer heavier cutbacks than others.

The next aspect to be stressed is confidentiality and security. If anyone other than the turnround executive's secretary does the word processing and copying, the information might as well be put on the company noticeboard. Detailed planning should be carried out to arrange for all severances to be notified and executed at the same time, so that uncertainty and anxiety among the remaining personnel can be kept to a minimum. Equally important, appropriate notification should be given to staff unions and government departments in accordance with the highest standards of custom and practice of the particular country.

Budgeting

The preparation of a budget for the coming financial year offers an opportunity to pursue further the installation of effective short-term management within the business. The management team has by this time had the experience of making a commitment for the current financial year and delivering that commitment.

The finance staff have been directed about the scope, methods and format required for financial planning, control and forecasting in the coming year and will be ready to implement this, starting with the preparation of the annual budget. Each member of the management team will be expected to back his or her budget commitment with a quantified management action programme and a statement of the key milestones to be achieved on business development projects. This will ensure that there is a balance between the amount of executive time spent on day-to-day management problems and that invested in pursuing projects to achieve further profitable growth.

A Worthwhile Future for the Company

Despite the effective implementation of headcount reduction, improved operational management and the initiation of business development projects, the anticipated return from the funds invested may still be unacceptable in the medium term, even if operating losses have been eliminated. The executive must not see the extent of the turnround role as being the elimination of losses. That is only the first step – and often the easier one. The second stage is to achieve an acceptable return on the funds invested, or to dispose of the business as a going concern.

If the requirement to achieving a turnround has resulted from long-term changes in the market place in which the company operates then it will almost certainly be necessary to re-position the business. This involves a planned withdrawal from unprofitable products, services, market segments and territories and developing or acquiring alternative business which offers adequate profitability and future growth. The re-positioning of the business can take place in several ways.

For example, the company could decide to look for future growth throughout, say, Europe; or it could concentrate on developing a higher quality, higher priced product range; or it could develop its ability to sell custom-made products profitably. A further option may be diversification to an extent which requires either a joint venture or an acquisition.

While the turnround executive may discuss ideas on the subject with other managers, and may well invite their suggestions, the responsibility for decision rests squarely on his or her shoulders alone.

In the end, the conclusion may be that the business should be sold as a going concern to another company better placed to make an acceptable return from the funds invested. If so, the turnround executive must have the courage to present the facts to the board for approval. It must not be seen as a statement of failure. In the final analysis, the management of opportunity is more rewarding than the management of problems, from the standpoint of shareholders, managers and employees alike. Once approval for disposal is given, then the turnround executive should expect to be actively involved, and probably personally accountable, for identifying prospective purchasers and successfully negotiating the sale of the business in conjunction with specialist advisers.

Throughout all this there will be uncertainty, anxiety and fear felt by workforce and management alike. The turnround executive must learn to cope effectively and be a person of integrity with outstanding management skills, and above all, the ability to communicate. It is important that he or she should appear cheerful, assured and poised at all times. If there are signs of despondency or being out of one's depth, the effect on morale may be shattering. Both management and workforce will look to the turnround executivefor confidence and reassurance. The executive's approach should be like that of the dentist who, at the outset, describes to the nervous patient the nature of the treatment he or she is about to receive and then explains each step.

Two other aspects of communication are important:

making promises and dealing with rumours. From the very start the turnround executive must not make any promises which are either beyond his or her control or beyond present horizons. It is not unusual to be asked on the first day if an assurance can be given that there will be neither redundancy nor office relocation within, say, the next six months. At this stage, the turnround executive is not able to give such an undertaking. The other feature of a turnround situation is the proliferation of rumours from top to bottom of the organization. Rumours must be flushed out into the open as quickly as possible, and an appropriate statement made by management. Rumours left undealt with merely fuel the anxiety which already exists.

In conclusion, it can be said that every turnround situation presents a unique set of problems. There are no ready-made answers. The outcome of a successful turnround is defined as achieving an adequate return on the total funds invested in the business, and not simply as the elimination of losses. The methods outlined for handling the situation successfully are based on taking effective executive action initially rather than concentrating on improved management control systems and procedures. The key to success is to concentrate on doing a few simple but important tasks outstandingly well, and to communicate confidence and reassurance to managers and staff throughout the business.

Key Point Summary

- Make an initial impact by eliminating, reducing or deferring discretionary expense items, for example: temporary help; personal cars and office equipment.
- Approve all recruitment because the aim must be to avoid hiring people at this stage.
- Start tackling the problems by spending time in the sales department, before assessing the market and

examining marketing activity within the company.
- Produce a financial operating plan for the remainder of the current financial year within 60 days.
- Carry out all termination of staff employment on one day to minimize the impact on morale.
- Remember the goal is to achieve an acceptable return on the funds invested, and not simply to eliminate losses.
- Concentrate on doing a few simple but important tasks outstandingly well; this is the key to a successful turn-round.

12

How to Make Successful Management Buy-outs and Buy-ins

Management buy-outs are commonplace in the USA and the UK, the largest examples running into billions of dollars or pounds. Buy-outs in continental Europe are becoming more frequent and a well established part of business life. This reflects the enterprise culture which is growing internationally and is being fuelled not only by the availability of funds from local institutional investors, but from the increasing appetite of large UK and American institutional investors to invest directly across Europe.

The American expression 'leveraged buy-out' is more accurate than the term 'management buy-out', because most of the finance is usually provided by institutions.

The members of the management team normally:

- Invest some of their own money, often borrowed against the equity in their homes or with the collateral of insurance policies.
- Obtain a significant equity stake in the company, disproportionately much higher than their personal investment of cash.

- Can increase their equity stake by achieving exit valuation targets, often referred to as a 'ratchet mechanism'.
- Have executive management control of the business, although the financial institutions usually appoint one or more non-executive directors to represent their interests.

In the UK, management buy-outs have grown rapidly (the largest ones having cost more than a billion pounds each), and more than 100 financial institutions provide finance for them.

Equally, management buy-ins have become commonplace in the UK. A management buy-in requires executives with a proven track record in a closely related market sector. The driving force behind the growth in buy-ins has been the large amount of funds available and a shortage of buy-out opportunities with a strong management team in place. This has developed inevitably into BIMBO (Buy-In Management Buy-Out) deals using a combination of existing managers in a business, strengthened by the injection of one or more managers from outside. Some successful buy-in teams have consisted of only two people, usually a chief executive and a marketing director. The first step is to find a suitable target company which can be purchased. Management buy-outs and buy-ins offer attractive opportunities to managers because:

- Financial institutions typically want to realize their investments within three to five years, by selling the company or obtaining a stock market quotation. If an attractive opportunity to realize the investment arises much earlier, usually they will want to take it unless the management can convince them of the extra benefit from retaining the investment longer.
- The record of success has been very high, but of course there have been disappointments and failures.
- Managers have multiplied their original investment tens of times in the most successful cases.

Buy-outs and buy-ins really do offer the opportunity to create substantial personal capital within five years.

The initiative for a management buy-in must come from the managers themselves, and many buy-outs also arise from the initiative of the management team. Groups are prepared to consider divestment, including management buy-outs for various reasons, including:

- The business is an unwanted part of a larger acquisition.
- It may no longer fit into the present commercial rationale for the group.
- The business may be too small to carry the overhead costs associated with a separate profit centre of a large group.
- The market is simply too competitive to carry the full weight of corporate overhead.
- The need to generate more cash or the wish to invest the proceeds in other opportunities.

Management teams need to recognize, however, that financial institutions are increasingly buying businesses as principals. They negotiate the purchase first and then choose a management team, which may be a combination of existing managers and people recruited externally. In this way, the financial institutions are better able to compete on price with trade buyers, because they offer the management team a significantly smaller equity stake than in a buy-out or buy-in initiated by the managers.

Other opportunities for management buy-outs, and possibly buy-ins as well, include:

- Privatization of state-owned corporations.
- Taking a stock market listed company private.
- An alternative to an unwelcome bid for a listed company.
- The purchase of a company in receivership.

Despite the availability of opportunities, and the substantial potential rewards, common sense demands that a hard-headed and objective approach is adopted by the management team.

Suitable Companies for Management Buy-out or Buy-in

The essential ingredients for a suitable company are:

- A positive cash flow
- Adequate asset backing
- The business
- The management team

Each aspect will now be considered in turn below.

Cash Flow

Cash flow is a vital consideration. Unless it is demonstrated that sufficient cash can be generated to pay the substantial amount of interest and repay debt finance when necessary, a deal is not possible.

It must be realized that the reason why the management team obtains a much higher proportion of equity than its members' contribution to the total funding is because a substantial amount of debt finance and overdraft facility is used to make the purchase. So, a business which is likely to need significant injections of cash during the next few years is unsuitable for a buy-out deal. This means that businesses in relatively mature industrial sectors are usually more suitable than those in young, high-growth and high-technology sectors, unless such a business can be managed in a way to generate cash: for example, by using distributors to stock the hardware and to install complex electronic systems which would require a substantial amount of working capital.

However, in that case, the distributors are making a sizeable share of the profit the company could be making for itself, but profit is secondary to the need to generate sufficient cash flow to service the debt finance.

Asset Backing

As a substantial amount of debt finance and overdraft facility will be used to finance the purchase, it helps if there are sufficient net tangible assets in the business to provide an acceptable level of security for the lenders. Service companies that are low on asset backing need to generate a strong cash flow as described earlier.

The Business

A suitable company must have a long-term future. The eventual sale of the business or a stock market listing could take up to five years. Then the purchasers or new investors will want to see continuing prospects. So the cash flow generated has to be sufficient to pay interest charges, to repay some of the debt, to provide for investment in replacement equipment and new technology in order to remain competitive, and to improve existing products and develop new ones where necessary.

The business may be making only a modest profit, producing a loss or be in receivership at present. This does not necessarily mean the company is unsuitable. A clearly thought-out plan will be needed, however, to show how sufficient profit can be achieved to help generate the necessary cash flow. Factors which may make this feasible include:

- Eliminating central service charges and providing the necessary facilities within the business at a much lower cost.
- Identifying specific and achievable cost-reduction opportunities.

- Defining opportunities to generate additional turnover from the existing facilities.

Significant amount of business with other group companies may be a cause of vulnerability. The management team should not expect favoured treatment as an independent company.

The Management Team

People talk glibly about management teams. Management teamwork really is essential for a buy-out or buy-in to exit successfully. Members of the team need to be a close-knit group, totally committed to turning their vision of success into a reality.

Investors look for credibility in the management team and the willingness of each person to invest. If the business is presently producing unsatisfactory results, the investors will want to know why and how the same people will be able to achieve a turnround. A competent financial director capable of ensuring cash-flow discipline is essential, but there should be no key appointment missing from the management team. If the technical director has just left, for instance, this may have caused a serious weakness and a suitable person prepared to invest in the buy-out must be recruited.

Making the Approach

Management buy-outs and buy-ins will be considered separately, as different approaches are required.

Management Buy-outs

The commitment of the chosen management team and their willingness and ability to raise some personal finance must be established conclusively at the outset. Otherwise, an unnecessary risk is being taken. The group may be upset at the suggestion of a management buy-out and even tempted to terminate the team leader if the business is not performing well. There is no point in taking the risk unless there is a determination to proceed.

One way to avoid this risk is for a specialist adviser to enquire whether or not a group is prepared to sell a business, without disclosing the identity of the bidder. This kind of approach is made frequently on behalf of corporate acquirers and is becoming increasingly common for management buy-outs. It is reasonable to expect the external adviser to make the initial approach without charge.

Management Buy-ins

A management buy-in requires a different approach. When an approach is made to a target company, the prospective vendors will want an assurance that sufficient funds are available before exploring a possible sale of their business. It is important that the management buy-in team has made contact with prospective investors before contacting a target company. In this way they will be more convincing to a prospective vendor and able to complete the deal more quickly. Additionally, some buy-in investors and corporate finance advisers know of companies which would be amenable to an approach, provided that a suitable management team is available.

Appointing a Corporate Finance Adviser

Unless the management team have previous experience of negotiating a buy-out or buy-in, and this is unlikely, they will need to appoint an independent corporate finance house or a major accountancy firm as their corporate finance advisers, to:

- Negotiate the purchase of the business from their present employers, knowing that if a deal does not take place they will wish to remain as employees.
- Select suitable institutional investors from the large number available.
- Present the management team, and their business plan, convincingly to prospective investors.
- Negotiate the best possible equity deal and ratchet mechanism for the management team with the institutional investor.

The benefits delivered for the management team by their corporate finance adviser should include:

- Making an anonymous initial approach to the parent company.
- Providing the valuation and corporation tax expertise needed.
- Taking a tough negotiating stance with the parent company when necessary.
- Choosing the three or four most relevant buy-out investors, from the dozens which exist, for the management team to meet and to make their personal choice of financial partner.
- Having enough experience to know how attractive a deal can be negotiated with the investors on behalf of the management team.
- Recommending a partner in a law firm with relevant experience.

The choice of institutional investor is important, for it involves much more than negotiating a one-off financial transaction. The investor will wish to appoint a non-executive director, possibly the person in charge of the investment or someone from its pool of available non-executive directors. It is important that the person appointed is compatible with the management team. Ideally, he or she should make a positive contribution to the business and not merely be a watchdog.

The choice of institutional investor will be put to the test if things start to go seriously wrong. The investor will want to see prompt and vigorous corrective action taken. In choosing among investors, therefore, the management team should ask how they have responded in situations where a company has faced a serious setback. The approach of different institutional investors varies widely: some are prepared to be patient, passive and tolerant, whereas others may seek to intervene decisively.

Timescale

Once a buy-out or buy-in has been agreed in principle, speed is essential, or the business is likely to suffer. Uncertainty may lower staff morale. Less attention will be given to managing the business whilst the negotiations are taking place. Typically, four to six months will be required to achieve a legally completed deal from the outset. Some buy-outs have been completed in three months, because of favourable circumstances. On the other hand, some deals have dragged on for much longer.

Business Plan

The purpose of the business plan should be to provide the information and forecasts for:

- Institutional investors to decide to invest.
- The target and maximum purchase prices to be assessed.

- The financial structure of the deal to be determined.

The plan should be written by the management team and must provide a comprehensive picture. The corporate finance advisers should provide guidance and review the plan to ensure that it is an effective document to help sell the deal to investors.

Investors do not expect everything to go according to plan, so they expect to see:

- Risk areas and uncertainties identified.
- Plans to address current or potential problems and to minimize their impact.
- Contingency plans if problems do occur.
- Sensitivity analysis to answer 'What if' questions.

The presentation of the document should be professional, attractive and readable; it should be bound effectively, and there should be an index. Published material such as product literature and press comment should be included in an appendix. The temptation to go into too much detail, resulting in too long a document, must be avoided. The first page of the plan should give a one-page executive summary of the entire proposal. All this may sound like common sense, but basic errors are often made. There may be no executive summary, the size of investment required may not even be mentioned and duplicated copies of published material may be difficult to read.

The content of the plan should include:

- An executive summary: a single page which tells the prospective investor in outline everything needed to know to establish their initial interest to invest.
- The company:
  - history;
  - present ownership;
  - location;

- key products and services;
- suitability for a buy-out or buy-in;
- commercial rationale for making the proposed investment.

- The market place, marketing and selling:
  - the size of the market place and forecast growth;
  - competition and a comparative assessment of products and services in terms of performance and pricing;
  - major customers and distributors;
  - marketing, selling and sales promotion plans.

- Manufacturing and distribution:
  - land and buildings;
  - production facilities;
  - use of technology;
  - surplus capacity;
  - need for additional capital investment;
  - key suppliers and sub-contractors;
  - warehousing and distribution.

- Technical information:
  - current and proposed R&D projects;
  - patents, licences and trade marks;
  - anticipated technological developments within the industry and the planned response.

- People:
  - members of the buy-out team;
  - organizational structure;
  - other key employees and expertise;
  - headcount analysis by department;
  - staff relations and any trade union or staff association involvement.

- Financial summary:
  - estimated purchase price;
  - anticipated time to realize the investment and likely exit routes;
  - working capital requirements;
  - historical and forecast profit and loss accounts and

cash-flow figures, covering the next three years;
– budgeting, monthly reporting and financial
management procedures.

The appendices should include the following information:

- Detailed financial projections of profit and loss and cash flow for the next three years, supported by a statement of all assumptions used and sensitivity analysis.
- Management biographies: factual biographies of each member of the buy-out or buy-in team and other key managers and staff. Qualifications, previous employers, positions held and tangible achievements should be detailed. Waffle should be avoided.
- Published information:
  - product and service brochures;
  - press comment and articles.

Negotiating the Deal

There is much more to be negotiated than simply agreeing a purchase price. Retention of a minority equity stake, the deferral of part of the purchase consideration, the structure of the deal, tax implications, conditions, warranties and indemnities may significantly affect the total cost and attractiveness of the deal, or even determine whether or not a deal is feasible.

The first matter for negotiation is to seek an exclusive option period. This means that an auction situation will be avoided, but it cannot be taken for granted If there is competitive bidding, the purchase price is likely to be higher. In addition, the added uncertainty may well damage morale within the company.

Key matters to be resolved, in addition to the purchase price, include:

- The use and cost of central services which will be needed for an interim period until alternative facilities are created within the company: for example, access to group information technology resources.
- Rights to intellectual property, such as patents, trade marks, trading names and licences.
- The cost of any redundancies.
- The transfer of pension scheme benefits.
- The structure of the deal and the tax implications for both parties.
- Warranties and indemnities.

In most cases, tough and expert negotiation is needed to achieve a satisfactory price for a buy-out or a buy-in. The burden of debt interest means that there is usually a fine dividing line between an acceptable purchase price and one which prohibits a deal altogether.

When agreement has been reached, the investors and lenders will require due diligence to be carried out. It is the due diligence reports, rather than the business plan, on which the investors will formally commit themselves to invest.

In the case of a buy-out, the management team's knowledge of the business, which it has used to prepare the business plan, should mean that there are no significant adverse situations revealed during due diligence. In a management buy-in, however, the business plan has to be written much more on an arm's length basis, so there is a greater likelihood that the deal is renegotiated or the financial structure amended as a result of the due diligence reports.

Staff

Motivation and morale should improve following a management buy-out or buy-in. There is a risk, however, that a 'them or us' attitude could develop, separating the management team that has invested in the business from the remainder of the management and staff.

Serious consideration should be given to creating staff incentive schemes on the completion of the deal. Depending upon current tax regulations, attractive incentive schemes may be provided by:

- Profit-sharing
- Share options
- Saving-based share purchases

It is nothing less than enlightened self-interest to err on the generous side when creating incentives for management and staff in either a management buy-out or buy-in deal.

Key Point Summary

- Consider initiating a management buy-out of your company, provided that a positive cash flow can be generated to meet interest costs and to repay some of the debt finance used to purchase the business.
- Consider a management buy-in of a suitable company in an industry sector in which the team have proven experience.
- Recognize that cash-flow management is crucial in any buy-out or buy-in.
- Appoint experienced corporate finance advisers at the outset to help negotiate the purchase of the business and to obtain the best possible equity deal for the management team.
- Consider setting up profit-sharing and equity incentives for staff at the outset to ensure maximum co-operation and commitment.

13

Selling a Business to Maximize Shareholder Value

This chapter is designed to help vendors gauge the right time to sell, to open a dialogue with attractive strategic partners in a discreet and confidential way and to ensure that they achieve the best possible deal for shareholders, management and employees.

Preparing for a Sale

Two questions need to be asked: 'Why sell?' and 'What are the alternatives?'

Why Sell?

There are various reasons why shareholders in successful unquoted companies are prompted to consider a sale. These range from individual shareholders wishing to retire or facing a succession problem, to a strategy by listed groups of selective divestment to focus on core businesses. Whatever the reasons for sale, however, there is one common and compelling priority – to achieve the best possible price for the company, structured tax efficiently, from an acceptable purchaser.

What are the Alternatives?

It is important that all the alternatives are considered before committing to a preferred exit route. Alternative exit routes which may be appropriate include:

- A stock market flotation on either the Alternative Investment Market (AIM) or the London Stock Exchange, or if appropriate an overseas stock market.
- The sale of a minority equity stake to a financial institution to unlock some capital for private shareholders, whilst retaining management control of the company.
- The sale of the company to a management buy-out or management buy-in team, or alternatively directly to a financial institution.
- The purchase of shares by the company to enable, say, a retiring shareholder to realize cash without the company being sold.
- The creation of an Employee Share Ownership Plan (ESOP) to transfer the ownership of the business gradually over a period.

For shareholders who wish to maximize the value of their business and find a strategic partner to continue the company's development, however, the right trade buyer can offer a large number of attractions.

The Sale Process - An Overview

Every sale exercise is different; however, the process always involves:

- A preparatory stage

- A marketing stage
- A deal management stage

These stages are addressed in greater detail in this chapter. In general, vendors should allow about six months from commencing the sale process to achieving legal completion.

Appointing Advisers

Vendors recognize that they can only sell their business once and the likelihood of achieving the best possible deal should be significantly enhanced by the appointment of experienced corporate finance advisers.

The principal function of any corporate finance adviser should be to take on the burden of project managing the sale, so that the vendors focus on what they do best – managing the business and maximizing profit. When selecting their advisers, vendors should seek the following:

- A track record of successfully completed unquoted deals structured tax effectively for the vendors.
- A worldwide potential purchaser research capability.
- An experienced director or partner committed to making the deal happen.
- The opportunity to obtain personal references by telephoning clients for whom the director or partner has sold businesses.

The corporate finance market is a competitive one and fees are largely comparable amongst advisers. Your adviser should be motivated to deliver a successful deal by making a large proportion of any fee contingent upon achieving a legal completion.

Grooming a Business for Sale

By 'grooming' a company for sale, vendors can significantly

improve both the likelihood of a sale and the total price achieved. Steps which vendors can take which will influence value include:

- Maximizing and managing profitability to demonstrate a steady and sustainable year-on-year increase in profits.
- Actively implementing opportunities for cost reduction which will not damage the commercial well-being of the business.
- Ensuring that the company's statutory and tax affairs are in order.
- Extracting tax effectively any surplus property assets with development potential from the company.

Finding the Right Partner

A key to maximizing shareholder value is to identify purchasers worldwide who have the most to gain from acquiring the company. The greater the potential benefits likely to flow from the deal, the greater the premium price which a buyer may be prepared to pay.

Vendors should identify buyers with:

- Complementary products or services but with a gap in their offering which the company could fill.
- An incomplete distribution network which the company can complement.
- And/or a geographical gap in their product or service offering.

Purchasers with any of the above qualities, together with adequate financial resources, should be shortlisted as worth approaching.

A large number of prospective purchasers are located outside the UK and it is essential to devote considerable time and resources to research on a worldwide scale to produce a short-list of known serious buyers.

Owners of private companies face a dilemma when attempting to identify and particularly to approach prospective purchasers. Whilst owners will be aware of likely trade buyers in the UK and perhaps some in Europe and the USA, they are simply not geared up to carry out a systematic search internationally. Equally, it is undoubtedly ill-advised in the vast majority of cases simply to deal with a single purchaser emerging from an unsolicited approach.

By the time an offer is negotiated at the heads of agreement meeting, the purchaser will be seeking binding exclusivity within a maximum of one week. This means that the owners are legally prohibited from dealing directly or indirectly with any other prospective purchasers. There is simply not enough time to solicit alternative offers before giving exclusivity. They will simply never have the opportunity to find out whether the offer negotiated is the only one which would be forthcoming or would be the lowest of several offers which could be received.

The empirical evidence, collected by Livingstone Guarantee over many years, is that when four detailed written offers are received at the same time, the highest offer is likely to be at least 50 per cent more than the lowest one, and in a significant minority of cases will be double or more. This means there is overwhelming evidence for selling an unquoted business by a covert auction process described earlier in the book.

One possible approach for vendors is to advertise the business for sale in the *Financial Times* for a UK business, using a box number. This is likely to produce between about 40 to 150 replies, from trade buyers, intermediaries and individuals seeking a management buy-in opportunity. To make the task manageable, it is recommended that a short-list of quoted companies and substantial private companies are selected as the most likely buyers at an attractive price. The other issue is that almost all of the replies are likely to be from domestic buyers.

Even if the owners of a private company are able to identify prospective purchasers internationally, the dilemma still remains as to how they can make contact without revealing that they are thinking of selling their business.

Consequently, the vast majority of owners of private companies appoint corporate finance advisers with appropriate cross-border and market sector experience to produce a short-list of known serious buyers. The process involves:

- A systematic international or global search, as appropriate, to identify relevant prospective purchasers, with adequate financial resources.
- The search to be followed by a telephone call with the key decision maker at head office, rather than simply the local managing director, to obtain the purchaser's acquisition criteria and to establish that they are serious buyers in reality, and not merely appear to be at first sight.
- Telephoning carefully selected venture capitalists to establish their interest in the opportunity as a financial purchaser, without revealing the identity of the company.

In this way, the research should produce:

- A handful of known serious buyers.
- A similar number of companies, where the fit is not quite as strong.
- A long list of names of rejected companies and the reason for rejecting them – based on the telephone calls to decision makers.

None of the companies will have any idea of the identity of the business being sold at this stage. Then the corporate finance advisers and the owners should agree the companies to be approached with the opportunity to acquire a relevant and attractive company.

Quoted groups are better placed to identify prospective

purchasers internationally and to approach them, using head office staff. In many cases, however, even major worldwide companies appoint corporate finance advisers to sell subsidiaries because:

- Advisers are geared up to carry out worldwide research, and should have relevant market sector knowledge and experience.
- The group may wish to establish the appetite of known serious buyers worldwide before finally deciding to sell a subsidiary and notify the local management – so it would be inappropriate for head office staff to approach prospective purchasers.
- Selling a business is time consuming and requires previous experience, so unless the group have an established specialist corporate finance team they will prefer to use outside advisers.

Valuation

There is no single correct answer to the question of how much an unquoted company is worth. A number of factors which will affect valuation include:

- The recent, current and forecast profits and cash flow of the company.
- The scope for the purchaser to derive significant synergistic benefits.
- The scarcity value of the company.
- The value being placed on comparable unquoted and quoted companies in the sector.

An independent valuation may provide an important comfort level for vendors who are uncertain of the likely achievable value of their company.

The true value of any unquoted company is not what the

vendor or a single purchaser thinks that it is worth; rather, it is the most attractive offer received as a result of several serious purchasers submitting written conditional offers to the vendors.

If a vendor company or its adviser can create a competitive bidding situation among a short-list of purchasers, the highest offer received is likely to be significantly higher than the lowest.

Marketing the Opportunity

The active marketing of any company to a short-list of purchasers is a highly sensitive process. Maintaining confidentiality within and outside the company is of acute concern to every vendor.

Marketing and Confidentiality

The risk of a breach of confidentiality can be minimized by careful management and control. Emphasis should be placed upon:

- Restricting talks to a short-list of serious purchasers who are known to be interested.
- Requiring every purchaser to enter into a legally binding confidentiality agreement.
- Drip-feeding information to purchasers on a 'need to know' basis to allow meaningful offers to be submitted.
- Not informing employees, customers or suppliers until the sale has been completed.

A purchaser's first impressions of a company are frequently based upon the initial information provided by the vendors. Particular care, therefore, needs to be taken to present the company in the most favourable light at the outset.

An information memorandum which provides an upbeat, pithy introduction to the company should be prepared and released to the relevant decision maker. Its principal purpose should be to prompt a meeting between buyer and seller — and no more.

Initial Meetings

Initial meetings with purchasers should be held on 'neutral' ground at your adviser's offices or a nearby hotel to avoid prejudicing confidentiality. Initial meetings serve two equally important purposes: purchasers should have an opportunity to meet the vendors and understand more fully the business and the opportunity it represents, and vendors should assess each purchaser to gauge their interest and decide whether or not the chemistry is right.

It is not generally appropriate for an acceptable price to be revealed at this stage, although the purchaser's plans for the company and the vendor's intentions following completion will clearly impinge upon a deal structure, which certainly is a valid topic for discussion

Site Visits

Vendors should normally be prepared to allow serious purchasers to conduct a 'whistle stop' tour of the facilities. Purchasers are often reluctant to make a written offer without having viewed the premises. However, such access needs to be carefully controlled by the vendors.

Vendors should accompany one or two members of the purchaser's team around the premises. Questions should be saved until a meeting is convened off-site immediately following the visit.

Following the site visit and provided the purchaser is still interested, limited further information should be made available on the understanding that a written conditional offer will be made. A key part of this information is likely to be the latest management accounts and a forecast for the next financial year.

Offer Letters

At this stage, purchasers should have an adequate understanding of the business to enable them to submit a written indicative offer, setting out:

- The price to be paid.
- The form of consideration.
- Details of any deferred consideration linked to future profit performance.
- Any unusual conditions.
- A timetable to completion.

Once written offers have been received from all the likely buyers, time should be taken to fully understand each one, requesting explanations where necessary and carrying out preliminary negotiation as appropriate to obtain improved offers.

Vendors should then decide with their advisers which is the preferred purchaser. This decision may not simply be based upon price and may include assessments of:

- Structure of the offer.
- Finding the best partner for the business.
- Deliverability of the offer.
- Chemistry with the purchaser.
- Timetable.

A second purchaser should be kept 'warm' in reserve if for any reason the preferred purchaser does not deliver.

Negotiations

The preferred purchaser should be invited to meet with the vendors with the specific intention of agreeing a mutually acceptable deal. It is vital for the purpose of the meeting to be made clear and for decision makers with the necessary authority to attend it.

Many vendors prefer their advisers to lead the negotiations as this gives them the flexibility to distance themselves from the 'heat' of the negotiations.

The outcome of a successful negotiation meeting should be 'heads of agreement' (sometimes known as a 'letter of intent'). The heads are a written record of the key features of the agreed transaction set out in commercial language, which can be used by both parties to brief the lawyers and other advisers to be involved in legally completing the deal.

Heads of agreement are not intended to be legally binding, with one important exception. Most purchasers will require the vendors to enter into an exclusivity period with them, barring them from talking to other purchasers.

Steering the Deal to Completion

Due Diligence

Due diligence is the process whereby the preferred purchaser and its advisers undertake a detailed investigation of the business in order to verify that it is as the vendors presented it.

The due diligence exercise normally involves the following areas:

- Commercial performance
- Financial performance
- Accounting controls
- Property and valuation
- Tax issues
- Legal issues
- Environmental issues

The exercise will involve the purchaser and its advisers spending some time at the company's premises reviewing original documentation, but as much work as possible should be carried out off-site.

The due diligence process must be controlled carefully by the vendors in order to guard against it being used as an excuse for renegotiating the deal and to ensure that confidentiality is maintained within the business.

Lawyers

At the same time as due diligence commences, the purchaser's solicitors should be circulating a first draft of the legal documentation. It is in every vendor's interest to secure the best possible legal advice and time should be taken to select solicitors who are:

- Specialists in the legal aspects of buying and selling companies.
- Willing to commit a seasoned partner to lead the deal from the front.
- Are prepared to offer competitive fees.

If the vendors' current solicitors have the requisite depth and breadth of expertise, their existing knowledge of the company will be valuable.

Legal Negotiations

Vendors should request first drafts of the necessary legal paperwork at an early stage to ensure that the purchaser is not being unreasonable.

Negotiation of the legal documentation may take between three and six weeks. Buyers and sellers often believe that, once they have 'shaken on a deal', their lawyers can take care of everything. This is a dangerous misconception and it is vital that both parties, and especially their corporate finance advisers, keep totally involved in the latter parts of the deal.

A large part of the legal negotiations will focus around the warranties to be given by the vendors to the purchaser about the company. This will require the detailed attention of the vendors, considering each warranty carefully and, where necessary, making disclosures against the warranties in a 'disclosure letter'.

Completion

Completion cannot come soon enough for many vendors. If the sale process has been managed effectively, vendors can be confident that they have truly maximized the value of their business whilst delivering it to a purchaser which will continue to develop it.

Key Point Summary

- Groom your business, before initiating the sale process, to maximize the likelihood of achieving an attractive deal.
- Appoint experienced corporate finance advisers at the outset to establish a short-list of known serious buyers internationally and to negotiate the best possible deal-tax efficiently.
- Choose suitable lawyers to work with your corporate finance advisers to steer the sale safely to legal completion.

Appendix: Checklist for an Investigation

Listed below is the basic information generally required in a pre-acquisition investigation. Whilst some of this information will be stored electronically, the owners are unlikely to give the prospective purchaser direct access. So information will typically be given in hard copy, with occasional supervised access to on-screen information to provide additional detail on particularly important aspects of the business. To this should be added any items which are relevant to the particular case.

Documents to be Obtained

Memorandum and articles
Annual return
Audit report
Tax computations, agreement reached, notice of hearings
Directors' service contracts
Pension scheme
Bonus and share incentive schemes
Typical contracts of employment
Agreements with staff unions

Land and building valuations
Loan agreements and charges on assets
Lease and hire purchase agreements
All agreements signed in the last year
Product catalogues, wholesale and retail price lists
Distributor agreements

History of the Company

Date of incorporation and important events

Share Capital

Authorized and issued
Present ownership
Significant past changes
Shareholders' relationships

Board

Other directorships
Interests in other companies
Relatives employed
Cars
Pensions
Loan of assets
Loan accounts
Other benefits
Consultancy agreements
Share options
Pensions to former directors

Assets

Land and buildings
- location
- tenure

- condition
- area
- valuation
- lettings
- surplus space
- planning status
- future improvements and potential for alternative use
- insurance cover

Plant and equipment
- value
- age and condition of major items
- capital expenditure – budgeted, authorized and contracted

Intellectual Property

Patents, trade marks and licence agreements

Other Assets

Investments in and advances to subsidiaries and associates

Stock and work in progress
- product group analysis
- physical stock check procedures
- valuation methods and past changes
- surplus and redundant stock
- provisions
- sale or return and sample stocks

Debtors
- age analysis
- provisions
- credit terms and exceptions
- status checks
- credit collection techniques

Cash

Liabilities

Loans and Debentures
- interest rate
- conditions and terms

Creditors
- age analysis
- credit limits and authorization

Taxation
- corporation
- capital gains
- PAYE
- VAT
- deferred tax
- tax losses available

Overdraft
- amount
- interest rate
- limit
- review date

Capital Expenditure
- authorized, but not incurred
- awaiting authorization

Supply Agreements
- sub-contract work in progress
- fixed term supply agreements
- outsourcing contracts, and termination arrangements
- unwritten supply agreements – and even important ones exist in this form

Profit and Loss

Sales Revenue
- product or service analysis
- key customer and outlet analysis
- territory analysis

- 'windfall' sales
- last and planned price increases
- discount structure and 'special' terms
- distribution channels

Products and services
- costing
- pricing
- profitability
- order book

Provisions
- movements in previous and current year

Number of Employees
- by department, at beginning and end of last year and today
- part-time, temporary, contract, self-employed or freelance staff

One-off Items
- accounting policy changes and non-recurring items in recent years

Payment to Staff
- typical salaries and wages
- company cars
- overtime
- holidays
- benefits
- bonuses
- last and next reviews

Pensions
- number in scheme
- number of pensioners
- last actuarial review
- discretionary pension payments

Accounting
- accounting policies
- budgeting
- monthly reporting
- tax planning

- cash and currency management
- staff
- contingent liabilities
- profit forecasts

Advisers.

Glossary

Controlled auction

A controlled auction is where a group or its corporate finance advisers announce in the press and other media that a subsidiary is to be sold. In the UK, the normal procedure is that detailed written offers to purchase the subsidiary are to be received by a given deadline, which is typically about six weeks from the announcement. Usually, a detailed Information Memorandum is made available and potential bidders are requested to submit their written offers without any contact with the management of the business being sold. Typically, between 10 and 25 offers may be received and then about 5 bidders are likely to be invited to submit a second round bid based on more detailed information being available from the data room (*see below*).

Covert auction

A covert auction is the method widely adopted to sell private companies by determining a shortlist of known serious buyers from around the world. The potential buyers will then be sent a brief Information Memorandum. They are invited to meet the owners and expected to submit their written offers at about the same time, so that an informed choice of preferred purchaser can be made.

Data room

A data room is used in connection with controlled auctions. No more than a handful of shortlisted bidders, selected from their first round bids, are invited to have access for one or two working days to the specially set up data room. This access is provided in order to give them the detailed information they need to make a second round bid, before a preferred purchaser is selected.

Earnings per share impact

When a large listed group acquires a small unquoted company, the impact on earnings per share is likely to be minimal. On the other hand, when a small listed group makes an unquoted acquisition which is sizeable relative to the size of the existing group, then it is important to calculate anticipated earnings per share of the enlarged group. The calculation will be for the current financial year and the next two financial years to make sure that there will not be an unacceptable dilution of earnings per share which could adversely affect the share price.

Indemnities

The share purchase and sale agreement for an unquoted company contains various indemnities, whereby the vendors indemnify the purchaser that in the event that the condition of the company at legal completion or any liabilities arising which emanated prior to legal completion, will result in their reimbursing the purchaser in full.

Niche Businesses

Many private companies are correctly described as niche businesses because they focus heavily on a specific market segment rather than a broad market sector and have either the leading market share of any competitors or at least a sizeable market share. As a generalisation, these businesses tend to attract a premium price when sold because of the attractiveness of their market share to potential purchasers.

Warranties

The share purchase and sale agreement contains a number of warranties. These are primarily a mechanism used by acquirers to ensure full disclosure of information by vendors concerning specific aspects of the business. Vendors are quite rightly encouraged by their solicitors and corporate finance advisers to fully disclose in writing, using a disclosure statement, any known breaches under the warranties in the contract documentation. It is important to acquirers to recognise, however, that whereas an indemnity provides for full recompense, a warranty requires the acquirer to litigate in order to prove that had they have known about the breach of warranty they could establish how much less they would have been prepared to pay for the business. So, whilst warranties are important to acquirers, their value is primarily in obtaining maximum disclosure and they should not be relied upon as certain means of obtaining recompense.

Index